A Case for Female Deacons

A Case for Female Deacons

JAMIN HÜBNER

FOREWORD BY
D. CLAIR DAVIS

WIPF & STOCK · Eugene, Oregon

A CASE FOR FEMALE DEACONS

Copyright © 2015 Jamin Hübner. All rights reserved. Except for brief quotations in critical publications or reviews, no part of this book may be reproduced in any manner without prior written permission from the publisher. Write: Permissions, Wipf and Stock Publishers, 199 W. 8th Ave., Suite 3, Eugene, OR 97401.

Unless otherwise indicated, Scripture quotations are from The Holy Bible, English Standard Version® (ESV®), copyright © 2001 by Crossway, a publishing ministry of Good News Publishers. Used by permission. All rights reserved.

Wipf & Stock
An Imprint of Wipf and Stock Publishers
199 W. 8th Ave., Suite 3
Eugene, OR 97401

www.wipfandstock.com

ISBN 13: 978-1-62564-884-6

Manufactured in the U.S.A.   10/24/2014

Contents

Foreword by D. Clair Davis | vii
Introduction | ix
Abbreviations | xi

1 The Argument | 1
2 Primary Premise and Conclusion | 4
3 Confirming Argument A: Romans 16:1–2 | 19
4 Confirming Argument B: 1 Timothy 3:11 | 28
5 Confirming Argument C: Historical Theology | 51
6 Conclusion | 79

Bibliography | 85

Foreword

I AM PERSONALLY MUCH delighted and encouraged by Professor Hübner's fine work on one of the most important issues before the evangelical church today: whether or not women may be deacons. The case has been well made before, by Robert Strimple and Edmund Clowney, but Hübner's work supplements theirs very well and speaks more vigorously to this generation.

The two main sections are exegetical and historical theological. His exegesis is characterized by its care and precision. Many have drawn negative conclusions from the biblical text without making clear the basis of their conclusions; Hübner challenges them at every point. I think this is bound to lead to significant progress as we explore this topic—if you are convinced this is not a role for women, you will need to answer his calls for precise proof. This can only be for the benefit of all of us.

He is especially skilled in contrasting biblical requirements for elder and deacon. This should help both sides of the question. Too often, ordaining women deacons has led rapidly to their ordination as elders, as witness the recent development in the Christian Reformed Church. But much more consistently, the Covenanters have enjoyed women deacons for well over a century without their taking the further step. Hübner's careful distinctions should minimize the emotion too often evidenced in this discussion.

Still, why did the Presbyterian Church from its beginning in America in its installation form of deacons include that the congregation should *obey* the deacons? Obey servants? What can that mean? Neither Hübner nor anyone else I know has addressed that

Foreword

question. It couldn't be simply quoting the Bible, could it, that the Lord calls upon you to care for the poor? I don't know.

The historical section is for me a newer area, and I suspect for many. Did we know that the list of Reformed theologians supportive of women deacons include Calvin, Charles Hodge, Dabney and Bavinck? (In my book the names of Strimple and Clowney are at least as meaningful). That information should also encourage us to look more precisely at the relevant texts, as Hübner has shown us the way.

I believe we all need more serious and prayerful work in this area. We know the value of "every-member" ministry, and there are certainly implications for women. As a seminary teacher I have had many, many godly and learned women students, and they have asked me how to best use their gifts. I've said: teach in a graduate school of religion, probably not in a seminary; find a place in para-church ministry, where the irregularity of para-church may cancel out the irregularity of women using their gifts; and become a missionary (pastor's wives are not pastors, but missionary's wives are definitely missionaries).

Hübner has helped us, but there is more work to be done. I hope especially that those of us in the conservative Reformed denominations may have meaningful conversations on the role of women with those now finally leaving the PCUS—but I'm not yet seeing it. Now, I encourage you all to profit from Hübner—and then go beyond him.

Dr. D. Clair Davis

Professor and Chaplain, Redeemer Seminary, Dallas, TX

Professor of Church History, Emeritus,
Westminster Theological Seminary, Philadelphia, PA

Introduction

THIS BOOK IS A revised version of my master's thesis, "A Case for Female Deacons," which I presented at Reformed Theological Seminary in Charlotte, North Carolina in spring 2012. The original purpose of the work was to persuade my complementarian friends of the legitimacy of having and publicly recognizing female deacons in the local church. This purpose has not changed, nor has the general structure of the argument.

Other than making the monograph slightly less academic in tone, I've made relatively minor revisions in the material, such as giving more attention to the origin of NT eldership, adding more references, correcting a few typographical errors, etc. Hopefully the work is more up to date, easy to read, and helpful. No argument is perfect, but hopefully this one is at least adequate.

It is unfortunate that those who seek earnestly to interpret and apply Scripture within even the most conservative standards of theology get thrown under the bus for writing a book such as this one. When various friends and colleagues heard the title of my thesis, some assumed I was on the path to liberalism, and it wouldn't be long before I would slip into theistic evolution, radical feminism, and general criticism of central Christian beliefs. It rarely helped to explain to such folks that female deacons have always been part of the Christian church and are affirmed by the very theologians that they most respect. It also did not help to point out that my position is the result of consistently holding to the same exegetical and theological standards as theirs. Alas,

INTRODUCTION

certain stereotypes and traditions about men and women (some alarming) die hard. Few welcome any kind of reconsideration.

It is beyond the scope and interest of this work to demonstrate that a case for female deacons in no way compromises a "high view" of the Bible or basic Christian theological tenets. I can only demonstrate my commitment to the Lord and to the truth by way of example—by producing cogent exegesis and argumentation in a way that serves the church and, hopefully, glorifies God. I pray this book is a success in that regard.

Jamin Hübner

Black Hills
Summer 2014

Abbreviations

ANF	Ante-Nicene Fathers
BDAG	Bauer, Danker, Arndt, Gingrich, A Greek-English Lexicon of the New Testament
BECNT	Baker Exegetical Commentary on the New Testament
BSac	*Bibliotheca Sacra*
CEV	Century English Version
DBE	*Discovering Biblical Equality*
ESV	English Standard Version
EvQ	*Evangelical Quarterly*
GGBB	*Greek Grammar Beyond the Basics*
ICC	International Critical Commentary
JBL	*Journal of Biblical Literature*
JETS	*Journal of the Evangelical Theological Society*
KJV	King James Version
LBCF	*London Baptist Confession of Faith (1689)*
LXX	Septuagint
NASB	New American Standard Bible (1995)
NBD	New Bible Dictionary
NET	New English Translation
NICNT	New International Commentary on the New Testament

Abbreviations

NICOT	New International Commentary on the Old Testament
NIGTC	New International Greek Testament Commentary
NIV	New International Version
NIVAC	New International Version Application Commentary
NLT	New Living Translation
NRSV	New Revised Standard Version
PNTC	Pillar New Testament Commentary
RBMW	*Recovering Biblical Manhood and Womanhood*
RSV	Revised Standard Version
TDNT	*Theological Dictionary of the New Testament*
TNIV	Today's New International Version
TNTC	Tyndale New Testament Commentary
WBC	Word Biblical Commentary
WCF	*Westminster Confession of Faith*
WTJ	*Westminster Theological Journal*

1

The Argument

IS THE CHURCH OFFICE[1] of deacon restricted to one sex? Since this study is aimed at those who hold the Christian Scriptures in high regard, we will first look at the biblical material and then look at how Christians throughout history have thought about female deacons. Each chapter of this book will correspond to a portion of the argument outlined below.[2]

THE ARGUMENT

(Primary Premise) The ban on women elders propounded by complementarians does not apply to women deacons; New Testament

---

1. Craig Blomberg defines office as "a settled or consistent function, role, or position" in Beck, *Two Views*, 152. Typically, an "office" also involves interpersonal accountability in the church and explicit qualifications in the New Testament. Belleville critiques Blomberg's definition on page 197 of the same aforementioned volume, calling it "anachronistic" precisely because the concept of "offices" was in development in the NT period. Thus, there were no "settled" or "consistent" church positions in NT times. Cf. Craig Keener: "We should avoid distinguishing between offices and gifts too arbitrarily, especially when someone receives a title as in Exod 15:20; Judg. 4:4; 2 Kgs 22:14; Isa 8:3; Luke 2:36) and our term for 'office' does not exist in Scripture (Eph 4:8, 11 calls ministers 'gifts'; 'prophets' in 1 Cor. 14:29, 32 seems to refer to any who prophesy)," 207. We will address this matter more thoroughly in chapter 4 when discussing Phoebe in Romans 16.

2. Note that 1 and 2 of the argument is in the same chapter.

teaching suggests that teaching and exercising authority over men is neither a required ability nor necessary task undertaken by a deacon (whether "functional" or "official"[3]).

1. (Primary Conclusion) Therefore, the office of deacon is not gender specific and qualified women[4] are encouraged to occupy it.
    a. (Confirming Argument A) The New Testament authors show awareness of women deacons in Rom 16:1.
    b. (Confirming Argument B) The Apostle Paul provides the qualifications of women deacons in 1 Tim 3:11.
    c. (Confirming Argument C) Female deacons ("deaconesses") are not foreign to the historical church. Rather, female deacons have been conceptually approved by Christian leaders and have actually existed in many churches throughout history.
3. (Final Conclusion) Therefore, the truthfulness of conclusion (2) is reaffirmed by the testimony of the Scriptures (namely, Rom 16:1–2, 1 Tim 3:11) and of the church.

You may have noticed that the structure of this argument is not like those that are often given in today's contemporary debates. Instead of assuming the burden of proof is on the one who believes in female deacons—and therefore puts all the weight on Scripture's explicit mentioning of female deacons (or something similar), I assume instead (in the spirit of the New Testament, I hope) that the role and function of church members are determined primarily by the gifts specifically given to them by God (Acts 11:29; Rom 12:3–8; 1 Cor 12:7–31; Eph 4:1–14; cf. Heb 2:2–4). If there are no real prohibitions or sound theological reasons against the idea of female deacons, and if the Spirit gives gifts to women that correspond to the task of being a deacon, then there seems to be every reason to affirm the legitimacy of female deacons. I do not believe

---

3. This popular (though often unhelpful) distinction will be addressed in chapter 4 when discussing Romans 16:1.

4. See Confirming Argument B for the qualifications of women deacons.

The Argument

that God gives spiritual gifts to people only to prohibit them from using those gifts—especially in the context of the church!

Thus, what follows from that point are "confirming arguments"—positive reasons to believe that women often ought to be deacons. These are the more popularly disputed controversies that surround the subject, such as the role of Phoebe in Rom 16:1–2 and the meaning of "women" in 1 Tim 3:11. Readers can determine for themselves how much weight ought to be given to each of these three cases.

As I said in the previous chapter, no argument is perfect. But hopefully it will become clear that, from an evangelical or reformed perspective that gives priority to biblical teaching, one cannot prohibit women from the office of deacon simply on the basis of their gender. One must look at a person's heart and soul—not their chromosomes—to see if they are fit to be deacons of God's church.

2

Primary Premise and Conclusion

> *The ban on women elders propounded by complementarians does not apply to women deacons; New Testament teaching suggests that teaching and exercising authority over men is neither a required ability nor necessary task undertaken by a deacon (whether "functional" or "official").*

ONE OF OUR MAJOR assumptions going into this work is that the New Testament generally teaches that church government is to be structured with elders (pastors) shepherding the church[1] and deacons ("servants") assisting the church.[2] This section of our study will briefly examine the origins of the eldership and the diaconate. We will then examine the nature of both in the context of the New Testament, and draw conclusions regarding the fundamental differences between the two to better position ourselves in answering the question: "do women deacons fall under the ban propounded by complementarians[3] of women teaching and exercising over authority over men?"

---

1. Apostles, upon which the church was founded (Eph 2:19–20), are (in the assumption of this work) no longer extant today.

2. For insightful discussion regarding of church government, and especially positive cases for a plurality of elders, see Grudem, *Systematic Theology*, chapters 46–47; Allison, *Historical Theology*, 588–90; White, "Sufficient as Established," 272–79; Engle et. al., *Who Runs the Church*; Thielman, *Theology of the New Testament*, 420. Cf. Beck, *Two Views*, 270.

3. See chapter 9 and appendix 2 in Piper and Grudem, *Recovering Biblical Manhood and Womanhood*.

THE ORIGIN OF THE ELDERSHIP

The elders of the New Testament appear to have originated out of (1) the need for organization and spiritual leaders for the local house-gatherings of the first century, and (2) the influence of Judaism and the elders of Old Testament Israel.[4] Three terms are used when speaking of elders in the New Testament: πρεσβύτερος (from which we get the word "Presbytery"),[5] ἐπίσκοπος (from which we get the word "Episcopal"),[6] and ποιμήν ("pastor").[7]

Exodus 3:16 indicates that a group of elders existed as early as the Egyptian captivity (seventy, according to Exod 24:1). J. B. Taylor picks it up from there in *The New Bible Dictionary*:

> It was upon this inner circle of seventy elders that the Lord poured out the spirit in order that they should share the government of the people with Moses (Num 11:25). After the wilderness period every city seems to have had its own ruling body of elders, whose duties, according to Deuteronomic legislations, included acting as judges in apprehending murderers (Deut 19:12), conducting inquests (Deut 21:2) and settling matrimonial disputes (Deut 22:15; 25:7). If theirs was a city of refuge they also hear pleas for asylum (Josh 20:4; but also see Num 35:24). Their numbers varied, Succoth having seventy-seven (Judg 8:14), and they are associated with other civil officials, [for example] heads of tribes (Deut 5:23; 29:10) and officers and judges (Josh 8:33). Maybe the term "elders" was a general word for the ruling body and included some of these officials. The national body of elders still exercised a considerable influence under the Monarchy as the chieftains of the people, having first agitated for the appointment of a king (1 Sam 8:4f) and having finally accepted David (2 Sam 5:3). Their position and influence were recognized by

---

4. See Reymond, *New Systematic Theology*, 897. Cf. Bavinck, *Reformed Dogmatics*, 3:341–42.

5. This adjective form is used 66 times in NT ("elder," "old"), and noun form (πρεσβύτης and πρεσβῦτις) are used 4 times.

6. Used 5 times in the NT, and is translated "overseer" or "guardian."

7. Used 18 times in the NT, and is translated "shepherd."

Solomon (1 Kgs 8:1, 3), Ahab (1 Kgs 20:7), Jezebel (1 Kgs 21:8), Jehu (2 Kgs 10:1), Hezekiah (2 Kgs 19:2) and Josiah (2 Kgs 23:1). Ezekiel in captivity dealt with them (Ezek 8:1; 14:1; 20:1), and they appear also in Ezra's time and in the Gk. period. While their authority was civil, by NT times the "elders of the people" (*presbyteroi tou laou*) shared with the chief priests the power of determining religious affairs and, if necessary, of expulsion from the synagogue.[8]

The term πρεσβύτερος is used for multiple Hebrew terms in the Septuagint (most often, "be old," but sometimes "great," "firstborn," or "chief").[9] It is also used in the following ways by first-century authors:

> Josephus used πρεσβύτεροι of old people, envoys, elders, and ambassadors and deputies. He used the word of the elderly and more frequently of a ruling body. In one of the Essene sects the elders were a ruling court that evaluated candidates for readmittance who were previously removed for violation of the strict Essene code.38 The community members as well as the guilty members were required to honor and obey this court. Consisting of no more than one hundred members, this elder court held to a stricter lifestyle than the other members of the sect. According to Philo πρεσβύτερος referred to the aged, the eldest of a group, ambassadors, the elders of Israel, the head or chief of a house, and the ancients.[10]

The transition into the New Covenant and possible overlap with the contemporary culture is summarized by Craig Keener:

> Certain officials in the Greek world, in both cities and associations, were naturally called "overseers." The Dead Sea Scrolls also use the Hebrew equivalent of the term for an office of leadership at Qumran; here it is probably equivalent to the synagogue leaders responsible for the synagogue service. This office is identified with that of elders in the Pastoral Epistles (Titus 1:5, 7), a situation that

---

8. Taylor, "Elders," 305–6. Cf. Waltke, *Old Testament Theology*, 590.
9. Mappes, "The Elder in the Old and New Testaments," 80.
10. Mappes, "The Elder in the Old and New Testaments," 80–92.

Primary Premise and Conclusion

had changed by the early second century (Ignatius *Letter to the Trallians* 3), but that still obtained in Paul's day (Phil 1:1; cf. Acts 20:17, 28).[11]

Thus, there are a variety of "elders" in the first century. There were those in the secular Greco-Roman world (mentioned above). There were Jewish elders who were part of the synagogue and Sanhedrin—the same ones who Jesus interacted with during his ministry (Luke 20:1; Matt 21:23), rejected and tried Jesus (Matt 16:21; 26:3, 47, 57; 27:1, 3, 12, 20, 41; 28:12; etc.), and often came into contact with the early church, for better or worse (Acts 4:5, 8, 23; 6:12; 11:30; 14:23; 15:2, 6, 22–23; 16:4; 20:17; 21:18; 22:5; 23:14; 24:1; 25:15; 1 Tim 4:14). And there were Christian elders (1 Tim 4:14; 5:17; Titus 1:5; Jas 5:14; 1 Pet 5:1, 5; Phil 1:1; cf. Heb 13:7)—who were either "elders" in a general sense of older, wiser believers, or actual office-bearers who directed a local congregation.[12]

Scholars disagree on the extent to which the more "official" elders of Titus 1, 1 Tim 3, and Phil 1:1 overlap the elders in the Jewish synagogue, and have been influenced by the synagogue elders. This makes it difficult to pin down the more refined concept of "pastor" and the "office of elder."

But the early church's conception of elder becomes clearer in reading the Scriptures themselves. Generally speaking, the qualifications of eldership are found in Titus 1 and 1 Tim 3:

> This is why I left you in Crete, so that you might put what remained into order, and appoint elders [πρεσβυτέρους] in every town as I directed you—if anyone is above reproach, the husband of one wife, and his children are believers and not open to the charge of debauchery or insubordination. For an overseer [ἐπίσκοπον], as God›s steward, must be above reproach. He must not be arrogant or quick-tempered or a drunkard or violent or greedy for gain, but hospitable, a lover of good, self-controlled, upright, holy, and disciplined. He must hold firm to the

---

11. Keener, *Background Commentary*, 612.

12. Bavinck, *Reformed Dogmatics*, 3:341–42. Cf. Glasscock, "The Biblical Concept of Elder," 66–78.

trustworthy word as taught, so that he may be able to give instruction in sound doctrine and also to rebuke those who contradict it. (Titus 1:5–9)

> Therefore an overseer [ἐπίσκοπον] must be above reproach, the husband of one wife, sober-minded, self-controlled, respectable, hospitable, able to teach, not a drunkard, not violent but gentle, not quarrelsome, not a lover of money. He must manage his own household well, with all dignity keeping his children submissive, for if someone does not know how to manage his own household, how will he care for God›s church? He must not be a recent convert, or he may become puffed up with conceit and fall into the condemnation of the devil. Moreover, he must be well thought of by outsiders, so that he may not fall into disgrace, into a snare of the devil. (1 Tim 3:2–7)

It should be noted that these qualifications are very similar to qualities "found in Hellenistic philosophers and moral theorists of the period," though with "qualities that seem particularly suited to running tranquil, just, and orderly homes, and to teaching right doctrine within the Christian assemblies that met in these homes."[13] It also seems evident that these texts are speaking of a more official, regular, and recognized role for the local church.

Another key text is 1 Pet 5, where elders are told to pastor:

> So I exhort the elders [Πρεσβυτέρους] among you, as a fellow elder and a witness of the sufferings of Christ, as well as a partaker in the glory that is going to be revealed: shepherd [ποιμάνατε] the flock of God that is among you, exercising oversight, not under compulsion, but willingly, as God would have you; not for shameful gain, but eagerly; not domineering over those in your charge, but being examples to the flock. And when the chief Shepherd appears, you will receive the unfading crown of glory. (1 Pet 5:1–4)

The scope of our study does not allow for a full exegesis of all these passages. But, despite various qualifications, what seems to remain distinctive in the office of the New Testament elder, in

---

13. Thielman, *Theology of the New Testament*, 420–21.

contrast to both the Old Testament elders (and, as we will see, deacons) is the ability to teach sound doctrine and to be able to "refute those who contradict" (Titus 1:9).[14] Elders, as the New Testament authors understand them (especially Paul), are those who shepherd the church of God by not merely having age, but by having spiritual maturity and the gift of teaching.

THE ORIGIN OF THE DIACONATE

Having briefly summarized the possible origins of the eldership and the basic nature of NT elders, let us turn our focus to the origins of the diaconate.

The word "deacon" or "servant" (διάκονος) is used twenty-nine times in the New Testament. In the ESV translation, it is rendered "servant(s)" eighteen times,[15] "minister(s)" seven times,[16] "deacons" three times,[17] and "attendants" once.[18] It's used as a subject three times,[19] an object ten times[20] and appears in the Septuagint six times[21] (only one of which is in a canonical book[22]). The verbal cognate "serve" or "minister" (διακονέω) is used thirty-seven times in the New Testament, and the cognate noun "ministry" or "service" (διακονία) thirty-four times. Clearly, the general concept of the word "deacon" relates to *service*.[23] A. F. Walls says,

14. "Differences between synagogue elders and church elders include the following: emphasis on the church elders' teaching role, lists of significant moral requirements for eldership, the lack of New Testament analogy to the ἀρχισυνάγωγος, and the lack of civil or political power." Mappes, "Elder in the Old and New Testaments," 92.

15. Matt 20:26, 23:11; Mark 9:35, 10:43; John 2:5, 9, 12:26; Rom 13:4, 15:8, 16:1; 1 Cor 3:5; 2 Cor 6:4, 11:15, 22:23; Gal 2:17; 1 Tim 4:6.

16. 2 Cor 3:6; Eph 3:7, 6:21; Col 1:7, 1:23, 25; 4:7.

17. Phil 1:1; 1 Tim 3:8, 12.

18. Matt 22:13.

19. E.g., John 2:9; 1 Tim 3:8; Eph 3:7.

20. E.g., Matt 20:26; Col 1:7–8; Matt 22:13.

21. Esth 1:10; 2:2; 6:3, 5, 4 Macc 9:17.

22. Prov 10:4 (LXX).

23. A *diakonos* is a servant/waiter (John 2:5, 9), a table-waiter (Mark 1:31;

A Case for Female Deacons

> In the majority of the 100 occurrences of the words there is no trace of a technical meaning relating to specialized functions in the church; in a few it is necessary to consider how far *diakonos* and its cognates acquired such a connotation.[24]

Context determines if the word *is* functioning as, for example, an "office" for Christ's church. One of the strongest indications that the term can be used in this way is 1 Tim 3:1–13 where the qualifications for elders and deacons are listed. The purpose of such qualifications, of course, is to establish responsibility and standards for a church-recognized position (office) that will remain normative for the church.[25]

What, then, was the origin of the office? There could have been a variety of influences, some (like the eldership) which are cultural. Thielman connects the qualifications of deacons with those of a first century general:

> A general should be prudent and not a lover a money, preferably have children, be the right age-neither too young nor too old—and have a good reputation . . . these characteristics are identical to or resemble some of the qualities in Paul's list. This is not surprising since one of Paul's chief

---

Luke 10:40), a "faithful minister of Christ" (Epaphras in Col 1:7), a minister of the gospel (Eph 3:7; Col 1:23; 1 Thess 3:2; 2 Tim 4:5; 1 Cor 3:5; Rom 12:7), and even the Lord Jesus (Rom. 15:8). Olson, *Deacons and Deaconesses*, 22. She concludes, "In summary, *diakonos, diaoneo,* and *diakonia* appear to have been used in a general way to refer to ministers, servants, ministry, and service in the church before *diakonos* was used to designate the office of deacon."

24. Walls, "Deacon," 261.

25. Cf. White, "Sufficient as Established," 272–79, and Towner, *Letters to Timothy and Titus*, 71. Towner says, "The codelike material of 3:2–7 parallels that found in Titus 1:6–8, suggesting that Paul may have used a traditional list of qualities for leaders." Guthrie, *Pastoral Epistles*, 195. He notes, "While there does not appear to be any uniformity in Paul's practice, there is no reason to doubt that he appointed elders on his earliest missionary journeys where occasion arouse. It is essential for Christian churches to possess some orderly scheme of government and the apostle had previously impressed this on his close associates. In the phrase *as I directed you* the *I* is emphatic, bringing out not Paul's egotism, but his authoritative endorsement of the elder-system." Cf. Mappes, "The Elder in the Old and New Testaments," 88.

concerns in 1 Timothy is to restore the tarnished public reputation of the church so that its gospel witness to those outside the church might be effective.[26]

Similarly, Walls says the term *diakonos* was used "in Hellenistic times . . . to represent certain cult and temple officials . . . foreshadowing the Christian technical use."[27]

Interestingly, Walls also argues that Judaism was *not* a major influence behind the diaconate.[28] This position contrasts with several scholars. Keener, for example, sees clear parallels between Jewish worship and the task of deacons:

> [The office of deacon] is probably parallel to the office of the *chazan* in the synagogue. This synagogue attendant was responsible for the synagogue building and would normally have been the owner of the home in which a house synagogue met. Unlike elders (3:2), this sort of "deacon" may have fulfilled an administrative function without much public teaching.[29]

Olson, in her thorough work *Deacons and Deaconesses*, concurs with Keener:

> Just as the elder and bishop might have carried over from the synagogue so, too, could the Christian deacon have been a carryover from the assistants or Levites in the Jewish temple . . . this "assistant" had evolved into an all-purpose employee, the *hazan*.[30]

26. Thielman, *Theology of the New Testament*, 420–21.

27. Walls, "Deacon," 262.

28. "There is little to suggest that in NT times the term 'deacon' . . . has any connection with the Jewish *hazzān*." Walls, "Deacon," 262. Cf. Lightfoot, *Saint Paul's Epistle to the Philippians*, 191–94.

29. Keener, *Background Commentary*, 613. One should note in passing that women who essentially functioned as deacons can be found in numerous places in the OT, such as the women who "served" and "ministered" in "the entrance to the tent of meeting" (1 Sam 2:22; Exod 38:8; cf. Judg 5:24). Cole, *Exodus*, 246. He says the position "probably stands for some form of organized sanctuary service, whether cleaning or sweeping."

30. Olson, *Deacons and Deaconesses*, 24. Cf. Mathew, "Women in the Greetings of Rom 16:1–16," 115. Susan's assertion in footnote 5 on page 109 is

A Case for Female Deacons

Perhaps, like the eldership, the diaconate could be influenced by both secular and Jewish influences.

As far as biblical origins are concerned, G. E. Ladd and others side with Irenaeus's second-century assertion[31] that the office began in Acts 6.[32] Contrary to Walls and others,[33] Ladd says,

---

somewhat confusing: "Paul (and the New Testament writers) preferred to use the [*diakonia*] word group to speak of service or ministry rather than the terms office or rule (ἀρχή), honour (τιμή) or power (τέλος) which denote positions of ecclesiastical office." This is not substantiated by any further argumentation (and such a string of assertions would require much; why, for example, is the term for deacon being compared to words that aren't related to terms that *do* denote ecclesiastical offices, like those for elders—ἐπισκοπῆς and πρεσβύτερος?). Nevertheless, it is true that "the [*diakonia*] a word group rarely functions with a technical nuance," as noted in *NET Bible*. Mathews also makes an error regarding "τέλος" which is not "power" (δύναμις), but "end," or "culmination." This is apparently a typographical error.

31. "Stephen, who was chosen the first deacon by the apostles . . . " Irenaeus, *Against Heresies*, 3.12.10.

32. Ladd, *Theology of the New Testament*, 389. Cf. Keener, *Background Commentary*, 338: "The idea here [v. 6] seems to be that of ordination, as in Num. 27:18, 23 (cf. 11:25), similar to the later practice for ordaining rabbis, called *semikah* (cf. 1 Tim 4:14; 2 Tim 1:6) . . . if so, the apostles considered their friends' office of social ministry quite important." L. Berkof gives four reasons why he believes Acts 6:1–6 refers to the institution of the diaconate: (1) the term *diakonoi* is used; (2) the ministry of these men is the same or similar to those elsewhere called deacons; (3) the requirements for office (1 Tim. 3) fit the tasks of these seven; and (4) the arguments for a later institution of the office of deacon are poor. See his *Systematic Theology*, 587. C.f. L. Keister, who asserted plainly in speaking of Acts 6, "the first deacons were all men," in "A Response to TE Sam Wheatley." G. Allison, on the other hand, makes two arguments that "urge caution in reading Acts 6 as the origination of the office of deacon, with the correlative division of church ministry into spiritual matters reserved for pastors or elders and physical and temporal needs that fall under the purview of deacons," Allison and Feinberg, *Sojourners and Strangers*, 242. Cf. Bock, *A Theology of Luke and Acts*, 387, who simply says, "We hear nothing about deacons [in Acts], although we do see a special group appointed to take care of a particular problem in Acts 6."

33. "[Acts 6:1–2] is commonly taken as the formal institution of the diaconate. It is doubtful if this has much basis in the language . . . the Seven are never called 'deacons', and secondly . . . while the cognate words are used they apply equally to the *diakonia* of the Word exercised by the Twelve (v. 4) and to that of the tables (whether for meals or money) exercised by the Seven (v.2). Laying on of hands is too common in Acts to be seen as a special milestone here . . .

PRIMARY PREMISE AND CONCLUSION

Apparently the distribution of food had been under the direct superintendence of the apostles, and the task had become so unwieldy that they were laid open to the accusation of partiality (6:1-2). To solve the problem, the twelve called a meeting of the church and had seven men chosen to superintend this ministration. Possibly this is the source of the later office of deacon. Paul's instructions for qualifications for this position suggest financial responsibility (1 Tim 3:8-13; see Phil 1:1). One of these "deacons," Stephen, proved to be a man very gifted in the ministry of the word (6:8ff.); but for the most part, the ministry of teaching and preaching remained the province of the apostles.[34]

Ladd goes on to assert that by Acts 11:30 the office of elder began to be formed. This assertion is similar to what R. Reymond concludes: "Deacons, first chosen to assist the apostles (Acts 6:1-7), were thereafter appointed to assist the elders."[35]

Indeed, Ladd claims that "there is no uniform pattern of government in Acts. The form of leadership was an historical development."[36] This development may have continued beyond the time of Acts. In the late fifties, when Paul's letter to the Romans is believed to be written,[37] Paul used the term in a variety of ways—such as applying it to a particular woman of a particular church (16:1),[38]

---

and the careers of Stephen and Philip show that the Seven were not confined to table-service." Walls, "Deacon," 262. Cf. Barnett, *Diaconate*, 30: "Their office was unique and was not continued in the Church." Additionally, Peterson, *Acts of the Apostles*, 235, states, "These seven were not ordained to an office, but were commissioned to fulfill a specific administrative task." The preacher and bishop John of Chrysostom also disagreed with Irenaeus. See Olson, *Deacons and Deaconesses*, 23.

34. Ladd, *Theology of the New Testament*, 389.

35. Reymond, *New Systematic Theology*, 899.

36. Ladd, *New Testament Theology*, 389. He holds that ministry was an "attitude of service before it was an office . . . Ministry was charismatic and not institutional." Bonnie Thurston, on the other hand, believes, "It may be possible to trace the development of this church function (or office?) from some of the passages in Acts, Rom 16:1, Phil 1:1, and finally 1 Tim 3:8ff." Olson, *Deacons and Deaconesses*, 25. Cf. Witherington, *Women in the Earliest Churches*, 113.

37. See Carson and Moo, *Introduction*, 394.

38. See Rom 14:4, 15:8, and 16:1.

and even applying it to Christ (15:8). By the late fifties to early sixties, when Philippians was probably written,[39] Paul and Timothy opened up a letter with an introduction to the whole church, but specifying the group(s) of leaders (or "offices"): "Paul and Timothy, servants of Christ Jesus, To all the saints in Christ Jesus who are at Philippi, *with the overseers and deacons*" (Phil 1:1, emphasis mine).[40] And by the early to mid sixties, when 1 Timothy was is thought to have been written,[41] the office was "official" enough to where Paul was willing to set deacons beside elders, complete with a list of qualifications for each.

DEACONS AND ELDERS COMPARED

It appears that the origins of the eldership and of the diaconate are very different. Although both may have had some Jewish and Greco-Roman background, they generally do not stem from the same elements within Jewish worship and contemporary culture. The reason for this is obvious: elders and deacons are of a different nature and purpose.

This distinction is apparent in the New Testament. Granted, the term "deacon" is used when referring to those who preach the gospel (e.g., Paul in Col 1:25; Apollos in 1 Cor 3:5; Epaphras in Col 1:7; 4:12), and cognate words are also used in referring to preachers (e.g., Timothy and Erastus in Acts 19:22). Nevertheless, "nowhere in the New Testament do deacons have ruling authority over the church as elders do, nor are deacons ever required to be

---

39. Carson and Moo, *Introduction*, 506–7.

40. "... the pairing of 'deacons' and 'elders' at Phil 1:1 and 1 Tim 3 suggests that the διάκονος was one who served in authority over a congregation but under the authority of elders/overseers. Confirming this conclusion are various statements by early Christian authors like Ignatius, who compares the relationship between overseer and "deacons" to that between God's will and his "command"—that which puts his will into effect," Agan, "Deacons, Deaconesses," 93–108.

41. Following Eusebius' assertion that Paul died in 67, the *ESV Study Bible* suggests for a mid-60s date, while Carson and Moo opt for "probably the early 60s," in *Introduction to the New Testament*, 571.

able to teach Scripture or sound doctrine."[42] Elders are primarily overseers and leaders,[43] deacons are primarily helpers and servants who assist in the ultimate goal of fulfilling the Great Commission and glorifying God.[44]

Nevertheless, even if one concedes that some deacons may exercise authority in some context (e.g., giving orders on how to set up chairs for an assembly), that does not mean the authority of deacons is the same authority as elders (i.e., same type of authority, same extent of authority).[45] Indeed, the exercise of authority in any church office is determined by the one who occupies it and the nature and requirements of the office itself. That is why the Puritan scholar John Owen can say the following:

> This office of deacons is an office of service, which gives not any authority or power in the rule of the church; but being an office, *it gives authority with respect unto the special work.* [46]

Orthodox Presbyterian professor Robert Strimple concurs:

---

42. Grudem, *Systematic Theology*, 920. Cf. Hamilton, "What Women Can Do in Ministry," 42; Clowney, *Church*, 233; Schreiner, "Valuable Ministries of Women," 220.

43. In some church traditions, greater offices are thought to include lesser offices. Wilhelmus à Brakel asserts: "For the office of the ministry includes the offices of elder and deacon, and the office of elder includes the office of deacon." *Christian's Reasonable Service*, 2:151. This is similar to Aquinas' words: "thus a priest can do whatever a deacon can: but not conversely," *Summa Theologica*, Part 3, "Whether Angels Can Administer Sacraments," Objection 1.

44. Agan rightly notes that, "only the omission of 'able to teach' from the requirements for deacons [in 1 Tim] gives us a substantial clue to the functional difference between the offices." Agan, "Deacons, Deaconesses," 97. However, Sumner, *Men and Women*, 243, is still right to assert that, in some sense, "A *diakonos* is a leader who serves." Cf. Frame, *Doctrine of the Christian Life*, chapter 33–34.

45. Contrast with Keister, who in arguing simplistically in "A Response to TE Sam Wheatley" conflates elder authority with deacon authority: "If there is authority wielded by deacons, then the strictures of 1 Timothy 2:9–13 come into play. The office of deacon is one of authority, and such authority cannot be wielded by women over men in the church."

46. Owen, *Works of John Owen*, 20:524, cited in Strimple, "Report of the Minority," 356–73, emphasis added.

The authority to be exercised by any church officer is that (kind of) authority which that particular office includes . . . authority of the deacon is not to be equated with the authority of the elder.[47]

D. Doriani agrees in slightly different terms: "Deacons lead, but they lead from alongside, not from above."[48] Therefore, it is an error to simply lump the two offices of the church together as if the nature and degree of authority for each is the same.

CONSISTENT COMPLEMENTARIANISM

Complementarians often explain that women should not be pastors because the authority that exists between man and woman in marriage extends out of the household and into the church. T. B. Madsen II explains:

> For Paul, male leadership begins in the home and extends to the church. The one implies the other, even from a practical standpoint. If women could serve as pastors in local churches, they would exercise headship over their own husbands, which Paul forbids (cf. Tim 2:5).[49]

But, this leaves us asking: why is one party of the family and marriage addressed, but the other ignored? Why are husbands analogically placed into an office, but wives are not? A *consistent* application of this principle would lead to something like the following (Figure 1):

47. Strimple, "Report of the Minority," 356–73.
48. Doriani, *Women and Ministry,* 183. Cf. Allison, who says in *Sojourners and Strangers,* 247, "Deacons and deaconesses engage in men's ministries, worship ministries, evangelism and missions, bereavement ministries, seniors ministries, singles ministries, sports ministries, fine arts ministries, mercy ministries . . . and the like. Because these ministries flow out of the office of deacon, those who serve in that office as deacons and deaconesses must possess and exercise the requisite authority to carry out their ministries. Their sphere of responsibility with concomitant authority is not the same as the same sphere of responsibility and authority as that of elders, nor that of the congregation. But they do possess and exercise appropriate authority for their office . . . "
49. Madsen, "Ethics of the Pastoral Epistles" 234.

PRIMARY PREMISE AND CONCLUSION

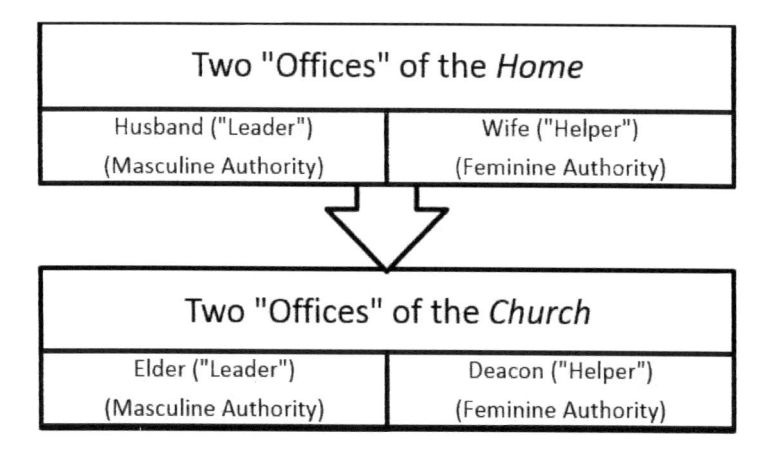

Two "Offices" of the *Home*	
Husband ("Leader") (Masculine Authority)	Wife ("Helper") (Feminine Authority)

Two "Offices" of the *Church*	
Elder ("Leader") (Masculine Authority)	Deacon ("Helper") (Feminine Authority)

This structure is not uncommon to the Christian church—past or present.[50] As will be addressed in chapter 6, throughout most of church history the situation was often that a local congregation had a number of deacons and deaconesses (female deacons) who assisted less numerous male elders or priests. Similar cases can be found today. Take Capitol Hill Baptist Church of Washington D.C., for example, which (in 2014) had over twenty elders and over twenty deacons, nine of who are "deaconesses."[51] Another example is City Church of San Francisco, which has numerous female deacons.[52]

---

50. White, *Pulpit Crimes*, 119, "What about the diaconate? What are the specific areas of ministry that would not involve the exercise of authoritative teaching by a woman over a man (Sunday School, women's Bible studies, etc.)? These are all excellent subjects for study, but they are often allowed to so cloud the central issue that the real problem is overlooked. Just as there is an order in creation, an order in the marriage relationship, there is an order in the ministries of the church. Despite the weight of Western culture today, God made men and women to differ from one another, and for good reasons. Part of the definition of the calling of the elder is to engage in discipline, rebuking, and the general exercise of authority in the shepherding of souls." But it is precisely this "order of creation" that speaks to the activity of women in church and, if consistently argued by complementarians, would legitimize female deacons.

51. "Led." Note that the leading pastor, Mark Dever, is an outspoken complementarian.

52. "Our Deacons."

PRIMARY CONCLUSION

2. Therefore, the office of deacon is not gender specific and qualified women are encouraged to occupy it.

Based on the foregoing argumentation, the office of deacon should not be regarded as gender specific. Qualified women may and should be encouraged to occupy it. Even Grudem, one of the most popularly known complementarians, is willing to admit this: "If deacons simply have delegated administrative responsibility for certain aspects of the ministry of the church, then there seems to be no good reason to prevent women from functioning as deacons."[53] The same goes for D. Doriani: "As long as we do not see deacons as authorities on a par with elders, there is little to quarrel over."[54]

---

53. Grudem, *Systematic Theology*, 944. Köstenberger essentially says the same thing: "Since being a 'servant' (deacon) does not involve teaching or ruling, there would not seem to be a 'compelling theological reason why women should be kept from serving in this capacity, as long as it is kept in mind that deacon is a nonauthoritative, nonruling ecclesiastical role," Köstenberger and Wilder, *Entrusted with the Gospel*, 25–26. However, it is a bit broad-brushed to simply assert that a legitimate woman-diaconate is contingent upon not having *any* kind of authority. As Owen and Strimple asserted, if deacons have authority, they have a *different* authority than elders. Furthermore, Köstenberger seems to suggest that simply having authority is something that women are not to do, or something that women are unable to have. That is certainly not the case given 1 Cor 7:4, the fact of female parents, teachers, etc.

54. Doriani, *Women in Ministry*, 182. Cf. Anyabwile, "I'm a Complementarian."

3

Confirming Argument A: Romans 16:1–2

> *The New Testament authors show awareness of women deacons in Romans 16:1.*

ROM 16:1–2 IS A hotly debated passage for the subject of women deacons:

> I commend to you our sister Phoebe, a servant [διάκονον] of the church at Cenchreae, that you may welcome her in the Lord in a way worthy of the saints, and help her in whatever she may need from you, for she has been a patron [προστάτις] of many and of myself as well. (Rom 16:1–2)

Paul applies the second declension noun "servant" (ESV, NET, NASB) or "deacon" (NRSV, NIV, NLT)[1] to a woman. It was common to use the term for both males and females since there was no first declension (feminine) form of the word.[2] But the general question is, should we think of Phoebe as a deaconess (a woman serving in the office of deacon) or as a general, less recognized

---

1. The RSV and NJB have "deaconess." The term is not anachronistic if it simply means "female deacon."
2. See Mounce, *Pastoral Epistles*, 202; Köstenberger, *Entrusted With the Gospel*, 25.

helper of the church? That is, should Romans 16:1 "be classed with Philippians 1:1; 1 Timothy 3:8, 12,"[3] or regarded as generic?

Arguments have been given on both sides.[4] The most common argument in favor for a more official/special meaning is the fact that Phoebe is said to be "deacon of the church in Cenchrea." As Clowney notes: "If *diakonos* were being used in the general sense of 'servant' we might have expected 'servant of Christ.'"[5] Schreiner also adds that "the designation 'deacon of the church in Cenchreae' suggests that Phoebe served in this special capacity, for this is the only occasion in which the term '*diakonos*' is linked with a particular local church." [6]

The *NET Bible* attempts to counter this point by saying,

> Epaphras is associated with the church in Colossians and is called a διάκονος in Colossians 1:7, but no contemporary translation regards him as a deacon. In 1 Timothy 4:6 Paul calls Timothy a διάκονος ; Timothy was associated with the church in Ephesus, but he obviously was not a deacon. In addition, the lexical evidence leans away from this view: the διακονία word group rarely functions with a technical nuance. In any case, the evidence is not compelling either way.[7]

However, this comment misses Clowney and Schreiner's point: there is something different about Phoebe in Rom 16:1 that does not allow the term to be understood only in its general meaning. Col 1:3–13, where Epaphras is mentioned, never mentions a city or a local church. The same is true for 1 Tim 4. Additionally, it seems superfluous to say that Epaphras (or any other Christian for

---

3. Morris, *Epistle to the Romans*, 529, footnote 9.

4. For an extensive bibliography of works favoring Phoebe as a female deacon, see footnote 6 in Gregory Perry's work, "Phoebe and Cenchreae and 'Women' of Ephesus."

5. Clowney, *Church*, 232. Strimple in "Report of the Minority, 356-73, argued this earlier: "If Phoebe's service being referred to were merely of a general character, New Testament usage would make us expect it to be linked with *christou* or *kuriou* or *theou* rather than with a specific congregation."

6. Schreiner, *Romans*, 787.

7. Biblical Studies Press, *NET Bible*.

Confirming Argument A: Romans 16:1-2

that matter) was generically "associated" with a particular church. (Was any διάκονος in the NT *not* associated with a church?) And in the case of Epaphras and Timothy, Paul does not command other Christians in their church to "provide them with whatever help" they need—something that Paul did do for Phoebe in the last chapter of perhaps his greatest written work (Rom 16:2).

Additionally, Paul also called Phoebe a "patron" (προστάτις),[8] which, although does not itself denote an "official position" in the

[8] The term προστάτις is only used here in the NT, and is not used anywhere in the LXX. Most lexicons and dictionaries define it as "helper," though at least one dictionary defines it as "protectress." The difference in meaning corresponds to the differences of meanings in its cognate verb "προΐσταμαι," as noted in Swanson, *Dictionary of Biblical Languages:* "1. LN 36.1 guide, lead, direct (Rom. 12:8; 1Thess. 5:12; 1Tim. 3:4, 5, 12; 5:17); 2. LN 35.12 be active in helping, engage in aiding (Tim 3:8, 14+), for another interp, see next; 3. LN 68.67 strive to (Tim 3:8, 14+)." Schreiner writes in *Romans*, 788, "It is very unlikely that Paul himself would say that Phoebe served as his 'leader' or 'president' . . . Paul is hardly enjoining the Romans to 'lead' Phoebe as she has been the 'leader' of others." This is possible given the context. This corresponds to the rendering of the verse in the NASB which, if correct, means the last phrase of verse 2 is connected with the helping of the previous phrase: "and that you *help her* in whatever matter she may have need of you; for she *herself* has also been a *helper* of many, and of myself as well" (NASB, emphasis added). In other words, if the αὐτὴ is properly rendered as an intensive "herself," then "patron" or "helper" must be defined in terms of the cognate παραστῆτε (*come to the aid of*). Thus, the meaning of "patron" is limited by the context, and Paul would essentially be using two words in v. 1-2 for essentially the same concept. But if the ESV, NRSV, NET, etc. rendering is more accurate, the definition of "patron" is not so limited and may have more possible meanings, hence Schreiner's first interpretation, and the interpretation of many others ("Undoubtedly Phoebe would be viewed as a leader in the church at Cenchrea because of her status and labor in behalf of the community," Walters, "Phoebe" and "Junia(s)"—Rom 16:1-2, 7," 185). Whatever the case, it is by no means inaccurate to say that Phoebe was a "leader," in some sense in the Cenchreae church, even if that leadership took the form of servanthood. This is suggested by Paul's command to others to give Phoebe the resources she needs to complete her particular (and apparently well-known and commendable) function in the church. As Mathew points out in "Women in the Greetings of Rom 16:1-16," 110, 114: "The lack of reference to teaching or authority in the list of qualifications of deacons does not imply that their responsibilities are limited to tasks of practical needs; rather to become the effective leaders in their household points strongly to their responsibility in the church (v.9)." Mathew also finds this truth about servant leadership elsewhere: "It is interesting that 1 Cor 16:15

church, continues to demonstrates her high status in the church.[9] As C. Kruse puts it in the (second) Pillar Commentary on Romans:

> It is reasonable to say that recent studies of the word [*prostatis*], and the fact that Paul's description of Phoebe both as a deacon of the church and a benefactor of himself and many others, is sufficient to show that she exercised a significant ministry in the church at Cenchreae in addition to being a patron of Paul's ministry.[10]

Additionally, the grammar seems to push away from a generic meaning as well. Perry notes:

> διάκονον is the predicate accusative in simple apposition to "Phoebe" (Φοίβην), made emphatic by the feminine participle οὖσαν in Rom 16:1. This type of appositional construction is used often in the New Testament to describe those who hold an official position (i.e., Caiaphas in John 11:49; Gallio in Acts 18:12; and Felix in Acts 24:1) ... while this construction alone does not offer conclusive evidence that Phoebe was acting as a church officer, at the very least it communicates that she was known as and characteristically functioned as a διάκονον.[11]

---

talks about the service of the household of Stephanas 'to the saints.' Service to the saints implies service to a group of people (gathered together as a church) and is probably related to a leadership role." For a brief discussion that favors deacons as leaders, see Frame, *Doctrine of the Christian Life*, chapters 33–34, and Sumner, *Men and Women*, 243.

9. Moo, *Epistle to the Romans*, 916. "['Patron'] does not denote an official, or even semi-official, position in the local church. The best alternative, then, is to give *prostasis* the meaning that it often has in secular Greek: 'patron,' 'benefactor.' A 'patron' was one who came to the aid of others, especially foreigners, by providing housing and financial aid and by representing their interests before local authorities. Cenchreae's status as a busy seaport would make it imperative that a Christian in its church take up this ministry on behalf of visiting Christians. Phoebe, then, was probably a woman of high social standing and some wealth, who put her status, resources, and time at the services of traveling Christians, like Paul, who needed help and support. Paul now urges the Romans to reciprocate."

10. Kruse, *Paul's Letter*, 556–57.

11. Perry, "Phoebe and Cenchreae," 16. Cf. Dunn, *Romans 9–16*, 886–87; Clowney, *Church*, 232.

Confirming Argument A: Romans 16:1-2

For all of the above reasons, it is difficult to justify putting διάκονος (16:1) in the category of "general usage" by translating it as "servant."[12] "Deacon" remains the best translation.

We don't know when Paul's ecclesiology reached a point where "deacon" represented what we commonly refer to as a church "office." But Rom 16:1-2 could be that very place. Indeed, Phoebe may be an example of the first "official" deacon[13] since this seems to fit with the situation of the early church.[14]

> Wilckens similarly sees here "one of the earliest witnesses to the formation of the diaconate," and A. Oepke thinks that this description of Phoebe "indicates the point where the original charisma is becoming an office" (TDNT, I, p. 787; Esp. if καὶ ... is genuine," as it surely is). Cranfield regards it as "virtually certain that Phoebe is being described as 'a' (or possibly 'the') deacon of the church in question."[15]

---

12. See Saucy, "Ministry of Women," in *Women and Men*, 174; Gryson, *Ministry of Women*, ch. 3-4; Dunn, *Romans 9-16*, 886-87. Cf. Walters, "Phoebe," 184.

13. E.g., Dunn, *Romans*, 887: "Phoebe is the first recorded 'deacon' in the history of Christianity."

14. Schreiner, *Romans*, 787, notes, "Women deacons were probably appointed early, especially because other women needed assistance from those of their own sex in visitation, baptism, and other matters." R.C.H. Lenski, *Interpretation of St. Paul's Epistle*, 899-900, is more thorough in his evaluation: "This is the first mention of women deacons in the church. The way in which Paul introduces this deaconess to the Romans indicates that the fact that women serving in this office was not a novelty but something that was already known. While we lack information we must, nevertheless, say that, since the arrangement of having male deacons in Jerusalem had proven highly beneficial at the very start, the appointment of women was the next logical step. The ministration of the first deacons consisted in the distribution of food to widows. But, surely, it must soon have become apparent that, for instance, in cases of sickness and of poverty and of loneliness, especially of poor widows and orphans, a need had arisen for the alleviation of which men could not be used; only competent women could serve in this capacity. Voluntary efforts would accomplish much, and in many churches they, no doubt, sufficed as they still do; but at least in Cenchreae we see the forward step, the addition of duly appointed deaconesses."

15. Morris, *Epistle to the Romans*, 529. The texts D* F G and m all omit καὶ,

We can never be entirely sure if the "office" of deacon was established and/or recognized in Romans 16:1 (prior to 1 Tim 3 and Phil 1:1), so we can never be absolutely certain that we should understand Phoebe to be in the same category. But, if there ever was a single, definitive point in time where the office of deacon was officially born (and that remains questionable given its historical development), it is certainly possible, if not probable, that Phoebe was the first to occupy it.

This leads us to a more important question: does it even matter, for our theology or for Paul's theology and the early church, if Phoebe was an "official" deacon? Certainly it was possible (just as it is possible today) for a person in the church to be *functioning* as a deacon without being *officially recognized* as a deacon.[16] Would Paul himself have made an issue of this? Would Paul himself have distinguished Phoebe as being an official deacon as opposed to an unofficial one?

Some people have accused Westminster Theological Seminary Professor Cornelius Van Til of having illegitimate scholarly credentials. One particular charge I recently heard was that Van Til never received a "real" PhD in Philosophy from a "real university." Why so? Because Van Til earned his degree from Princeton University in 1927, and the school (I was told) wasn't accredited until after 1927. Therefore, Van Til should not be recognized as a philosopher or scholar, because, *technically*, he never held an accredited doctoral degree.

I later found out that Princeton University *was* accredited at the time of Van Til's matriculation (1921 and following). But, let's say it wasn't. Let's say this charge was correct and that Van Til's PhD was from an unaccredited Princeton University. Princeton's education didn't radically change from 1920 to 1921. 1921 is simply the year that a particular accrediting institution decided to *recognize* the status of their extant education. Van Til would be

---

but this isn't a great witness compared to those texts that include καὶ (e.g., ℵ B C D Ψ 33 maj.)

16. In fact, it could be argued that most churches have more functioning deacons than official deacons.

no more of a "scholar" or "philosopher" if he had graduated from an accredited Princeton University than an unaccredited Princeton University from a year earlier. "Official," then, can be a bit of an overrated term.

Similarly, there is a sense in which Phoebe would be no more of a "deacon" if she was officially recognized by the church (whatever this means) than unofficially recognized or even nonrecognized by the same church. She functioned as a deacon in any case. And being that she *was* singled out and called a "deacon" by an apostle, it's hard to see what more needs to be verified. As Clowney wisely puts it:

> How do we define "office" if not as a function that requires public recognition for its proper exercise? If Paul had not called Phoebe a *diakonos* at all, the fact of his commending her for support by the Roman church in her work indicates that she was entitled to formal recognition in any case.[17]

Herman Ridderbos raises a similar concern:

> Even if Phoebe were not a deaconess in the "official" sense of the word, there is in that fact, as we have repeatedly contended, no fundamental difference whatever from official appointment to the occupancy of such a ministry by the church. Nor is there any argument whatever to be derived from Paul's epistles that it was only a non-official *charisma* that was extended to the woman and not regular office.[18]

---

17. Clowney, *Church*, 232. Perhaps Clowney is agreeing with Liefield, as perhaps we might all agree: "Function is more important than office." See Liefield, "Nature of Authority," 268.

18. Ridderbos, *Paul*, 461. This is similar to Murray's assertion on this text in *Epistle to the Romans*, 2:226: "there is no more warrant to posit an *office* than in the case of the widows who, prior to their becoming in charge of the church, must have borne the features mentioned in 1 Tim 5:9, 10." Cf. Belleville, *Two Views*, 197, who goes as far as to say "there is nothing settled or consistent about leadership in the early church apart from the possession of leadership gifts, whether it was Italy (Rom 12:4-8), Asia Minor (Eph 4:7-13), or Greece (1 Cor 12:7-12, 27-30). Yes, the apostle Paul appointed elders as part of the church-planting process in Asia (Acts 14:23); cf. 1 Pet 1:1; 5:1-4). But there is

Indeed, it is hard to see how Rom 16:1–2 can truly be distinguished from such texts as 1 Tim 3 and Phil 1:1 since in all three the church publicly recognizes a particular position with certain (stated or unstated) responsibilities in the church. That is what an "office" is. It would also be odd if Paul was praising someone who didn't actually meet the qualifications for being a deacon (1 Tim 3).

In conclusion, Phoebe was either an "official" deacon in the same sense as 1 Tim 3 and Phil 1:1, or would certainly be recognized as one once the "office" developed in the ongoing progress of the early church.[19] Thus, D. Moo and C. H. Dodd probably summarize the text the best:

> But the qualification of "diakonos" by "of the church" suggests, rather, that Phoebe held at Cenchreae the "office" of "deacon" as Paul describes it in 1 Tim 3:8–12 (cf. Phil. 1:1). We put "office" in quotation marks because it is very likely that regular offices in local Christian churches were still in the process of being established, as people who regularly ministered in a certain way were gradually

---

no indication he did so in Greece. There is no mention of elders (or any other settled function) in the church at Corinth. Ephesian church leaders are called *elders* (Acts 20:17; cf. 1 Pet 5:1). But the Philippian leaders are identified as *overseers* and *deacons*—with no elders in sight. Phoebe is identified as a *deacon* of the Cenchraean church, Paul urges the Thessalonians to respect those who work hard among them, and the Roman church had many leaders Paul recognized as *coworkers* and *colaborers*. But the language of *elder, deacon,* and *overseer* is missing entirely."

19. This is true even if the primary semantic domain of the term used in the text may be referring to "envoy" or "representative." This is Agas' conclusion. He says in "Deacons, Deaconesses," 106–07, "In terms of the contemporary church, we may compare this scenario to a female seminarian's urging a church in the U.S. to support the work of her home church in another country; to having a female member of a congregation speak as a representative of that congregation to another church's session; or to having a woman from one church encourage another church (or presbytery) to embrace a ministry that has begun to flourish in her own congregation." However, it is still difficult to see why this interpretation, if this is how Phoebe is being referred to in Rom 16:1–2, precludes her from being a "deacon" (or "pre-deacon," see quote of Moo) in the sense of 1 Tim 3:11. Certainly "envoy" is (or at least can be) just one type of diaconate ministry.

Confirming Argument A: Romans 16:1-2

recognized officially by the congregation and given a regular title.[20]

And Dodd:

> Whatever the "deacons" were at Philippi, that Phoebe was at Cenchrea.[21]

---

20. Moo, *Epistle to the Romans*, 914. Cf. Denney, *St. Paul's Epistle*, 2:717–18.
21. Dodd cited in Walters, "Phoebe," 185.

4

Confirming Argument B: 1 Timothy 3:11

> *The New Testament authors show awareness of women deacons in 1 Timothy 3:11.*

THIS CHAPTER WILL ARGUE that the "women" of 1 Tim 3:11 are female deacons, and thus support our overarching argument.

> Deacons likewise must be dignified, not double-tongued, not addicted to much wine, not greedy for dishonest gain. (9) They must hold the mystery of the faith with a clear conscience. (10) And let them also be tested first; then let them serve as deacons if they prove themselves blameless. (11) [γυναῖκας] likewise must be dignified, not slanderers, but sober-minded, faithful in all things. (12) Let deacons each be the husband of one wife, managing their children and their own households well. (13) For those who serve well as deacons gain a good standing for themselves and also great confidence in the faith that is in Christ Jesus. (1 Tim 3:8–13)

The major debate over this text is whether γυναῖκας ("wives"/"women") should be understood as deacons' wives or as women deacons.[1] Many arguments have been made for both sides.

---

1. There are other minority views, such as that the women are assistants to deacons. But it will become clear that this option is also unlikely. In any case, note the following renderings: "the women" and "women," in the NASB, NRSV, NIV2011, TNIV (2005), AMP, ASV, CEV, RSV, and Barclay; "the

Confirming Argument B: 1 Timothy 3:11

Many do not take an interpretation and leave the matter open for debate.[2]

The reasons for interpreting these women as women deacons have been commonly grouped in lists of three to five items. Among dozens of theologians and exegetes, seven notable scholars have given such lists: R. Saucy,[3] A. Köstenberger,[4] T. Schreiner,[5] E. Clowney,[6] J. MacArthur,[7] J. Piper,[8] and P. Towner.[9] It appears that most of these scholars build off Cerling's 1976 *JETS* essay, "Women Ministers in the New Testament Church?"[10] But it is certainly possible that they came to their conclusions without having read Cerling's work.

Since there is substantial overlap between these arguments, I'll summarize them in six points:

1. There are no parallel qualifications for elders' wives in 1 Tim 3:1–7[11] (and given the seriousness and lengthier quali-

---

women deacons," in a footnote for the NLT; "the women who are deacons," in the TNIV (2001); "women in this office," in the REB; "their wives," in the ESV, NET, NKJV, KJV, NIV (1984).

2. See Carson and Moo, *Introduction to the New Testament*, 571, 576, and Keener, *Background Commentary*, 613.

3. Saucy, "Ministry of Women," in *Women and Men*, 175.

4. Köstenberger, "Hermeneutical and Exegetical Challenges" in *Entrusted with the Gospel*, 25; "New Testament Pattern of Church Government." Midwestern Lecture #3. http://www.biblicalfoundations.org/pdf/pdfarticles/midwestern_3.pdf.

5. Schreiner, "Valuable Ministries of Women," 213–14.

6. Clowney, *Church*, 233.

7. MacArthur, *1 Timothy*, 130.

8. Piper, "What Did Deacons Do?"

9. Towner, *Letters to Timothy and Titus*, 266. Cf. Hurley, who said in 1981 in *Man and Woman*, 232: "I conclude, then, that 1 Tim 3:1–11 sets out qualifications for three groups of persons: bishops (elders), deacons, and women who probably served as deacons as well."

10. Sterling, "Women Ministers," 209–15.

11. Perry, "Phoebe and Cenchreae," 9–36: "If Paul was listing character requirements for the 'wives' of deacons in 3:11, then why did he not list any such requirements for the 'wives' of overseers in 3:2–7, especially in light of the fact that overseers must be hospitable? Though Calvin suggested that 3:11 may

fications for that position, we would expect that something would be said of their wives[12]).

2. There is no possessive pronoun ("their") or article used to indicate that the relationship to the deacons is one of marriage; "women" has no modifiers, and so the placement of "the women" in the context becomes important in understanding who they are (see point 3 below).[13]

3. The requirements listed for the women in 3:11 are almost identical to those for deacons in general (3:8-10). The similarities are due to the same office, the differences due to addressing more gender-specific concerns in the office-bearer.

4. The structure and form of the text.

    a. There was no distinct feminine form of the word for deacon during the time of the New Testament. If the Apostle Paul mentioned female deacons, he had two ways to do this: (1) use the generic term (διάκονος) and apply it to a specific woman who did such work (as he does in Rom 16:1), or (2) use the term generic "women" in the middle of a general discussion on deacons, even if this risked interrupting the flow of the text. In this case, helping words would need to be supplied (e.g., "likewise," ὡσαύτως) so that the distinctiveness of these women is retained.

---

be speaking of the "wives" of both overseers and deacons, this possibility must be ruled out by the fact that 3:11 is matted within the character requirements for deacons, framed between 3:8-10 and 3:12-13, which repeatedly reference "deacons" (διάκονοι; 3:8, 12) and «serving as a deacon» (διακονέω; 3:10,13)."

12. Blackburn, "Identity of the 'Women,'" 308: "One might argue cogently that 'unsuitable behavior' by a bishop's wife . . . has even more potential for undermining the church's life and work than the misbehavior of a deacon's spouse."

13. MacArthur, *Answering Key Questions*, "Contrary to the King James Version's translation of that verse, we know Paul was not talking about the wives of deacons because he used no pronoun to refer to them. He didn't say *their* wives, or *their* women. Also, since there are no comments about the wives of elders, why would there be any comments about the wives of deacons?"

Confirming Argument B: 1 Timothy 3:11

b. The first option is obviously not used (e.g., we have no names of the women he's referring to).

c. The only option left is (2). By inserting "the women" in a somewhat abrupt way (i.e., by introducing it with "likewise" and inserting into the flow of a text primarily about male deacons), and by so closely aligning the qualifications of female deacons with those of male deacons, Paul is able to distinguish the two types while at the same grouping them together.[14]

d. So the structure and particular content of the passage is explained by the fact that Paul is trying to establish the qualifications for deacons who happen to be women. No other interpretation better explains why (1) Paul used ὡσαύτως in the way he did and (2) why he placed the qualifications for these women in the particular place in the text that he did.[15]

Barry Blackburn adds two related points worth noting:

5. Statistical analysis of the use of γυνή strongly weights against a "wives of deacons" rendering.

---

14. See Bruce, *Romans*, 252.

15. Köstenberger, *Entrusted with the Gospel*, 24: "Structurally, the presence of the phrase 'likewise' or 'in the same way' ... in 1 Tim 3:8 and 11 may suggest that qualifications are given for two other types of officeholders besides that of overseer (3:1–7). The flow of thought in 3:8–13 may indicate that one large category, that of deacon, is discussed, with Paul first addressing qualifications for male and then female office-holders, with a final verse being devoted to a concluding comment regarding male deacons and a general statement pertaining to deacons in general." Perry's argument for syntactical structure is different from Köstenberger's, as he compares 1 Tim 2 with 1 Tim 3. But his conclusion is nevertheless the same: "Based on Paul's alternating pattern of addressing 'men' then 'women' in 1 Tim 2, the clear syntactical parallel between 2:9 and 3:11 (ὡσαύτως γυναῖκας and γυναῖκας ὡσαύτως), the coherence of the whole and tight framing of 3:11 within the discussion about 'deacons' (3:8–13), I conclude that the 'women' Paul describes in 3:11 are women candidates for diaconal service or 'women deacons.'" Perry, "Phoebe of Cenchreae," 33. For a popular summary, see Cunningham and Hamilton, *Why Not Women?*, 229.

6. The virtually identical qualifications between deacons in verse eight and "women" in verse eleven, is best explained by understanding the women in question as female deacons: "while one could conceive of some attention being given to the character of bishops' and deacons' wives in a unit *following* verses 1–13, there is no discernible reason why such qualifications should appear *within* a paragraph concerned with deacons."[16] In other words, not only are the qualification similar, but the placement and structure of the qualifications with verse eleven lends support to an interpretation of women-deacons.

When taken cumulatively, these reasons present a strong case that when Paul mentions "the women" in 1 Tim 3:11, he is discussing women deacons. Combined with the numerous women that Paul went out of his way to thank for their work in ministry (e.g., Rom 16:1–16, Phil 4:2), it becomes more and more reasonable.

SCHREINER'S FIVE POSSIBLE OBJECTIONS

Nevertheless, a host of objections have been raised against these arguments. Thomas Schreiner provides five possible reasons why the text *might not* be referring to women deacons.

The first is that "the qualification 'husband of but one wife' in 1 Tim 3:12 would naturally exclude women."[17] But, 1 Tim 3 also requires managing "children well." Unless we are willing to say that Paul's qualification prohibits non-married, childless men from being deacons (and elders for that matter), we must also admit that it does not necessarily exclude women.[18] Indeed, "Paul is speaking of the ordinary cases and

---

16. Blackburn, "Identity of the 'Women,'" 305.

17. Schreiner, "Valuable Ministries of Women," 505, footnote 13.

18. In "Can an Elder be Divorced?" Mounce writes, "Some hold that it means an elder must be married. But the force of the construction places its emphasis on "one" (because of its location at the beginning of the phrase), makes Timothy and Paul ineligible for eldership, and runs counter to Paul's preference for celibacy." Cf. Towner, *Letters to Timothy and Titus*, 250–51, and

is not absolutely requiring marriage or children"[19] or maleness, especially since he goes out of his way (quite literally) to talk about "women" in the foremost text on the qualifications for deacons in the NT.

The second reason Schreiner provides is that "since the subject in verses 8–10 and 12–13 is male deacons, it would be unusual to switch the subject to female deacons in the middle of the discussion (verse 11) without giving explicit indication of that fact by some phrase such as "the women *who serve as deacons* likewise must be serious."[20] This argument is essentially the same as Reymond's second objection and Grudem's first objection in their systematic theologies.[21] But, clearly "women" is as equally unusual to be found in this context, regardless if they are deacons or deacons' wives. The fact is, neither interpreting the text as "deacons' wives" or "women deacons" gets rid of the general fact of oddity.[22] It is unusual that Paul would exclude "their" if he were talking about deacons' wives and it is unusual that Paul would exclude "who serve as deacons" if he were talking of women deacons. And, contrary to what Schreiner has asserted, Paul *does* give an explicit indication that he may be shifting gears—the adverb "likewise" (ὡσαύτως).

The third objection Schreiner mentions is that if the text were speaking of women deacons, "a requirement for the wives of deacons would be appropriate in this context, since Paul sees the status and conduct of a man's family as an essential qualification

---

Towner and Marshall, *Critical and Exegetical Commentary*, 154–56.

19. 1 Tim 3:2–3. Paul would have had similar requirements for women regarding husbands were it not for the fact that in "ordinary" cases no woman would be married to more than one man. And it is probable that the female deaconesses in the early church were single (in fact, it wouldn't be long and the church would require celibacy for church officers; see chapter 6). See chapter 4 on Phoebe.

20. Schreiner, *RBMW*, 505, footnote 13.

21. Grudem, *Systematic Theology*, 919, footnote 25; Reymond, *New Systematic Theology*, 901, footnote 10.

22. The *ESV Study Bible* says on 3:11: "These women appear abruptly in the flow of the text," and Towner comments, "Rather abruptly the focus shifts momentarily from male deacons to 'the women [who are deacons],'" *Letters to Timothy and Titus*, 265.

for church office (1 Tim 3:2, 4–5, 12)."[23] Grudem raises a similar objection.[24] While Schreiner raises a significant point, it only accentuates the problem that qualifications for elders' wives are excluded altogether from the qualifications for elders in both 1 Timothy 3 and Titus 1, compelling us again to think these women aren't merely the wives of deacons after all.

The fourth potential reason Schreiner provides against women deacons in 1 Tim 3 is that "The word *likewise* . . . in verse eleven does not necessarily prove that women were deacons, because Paul may be commanding the wives to have the same virtues as male deacons without implying that they shared the same office." Schreiner is correct; the use of "likewise" doesn't in itself necessarily prove anything.[25] But when combined with other factors in the immediate context, its use supports the idea that the women in question were deacons. And, as we briefly saw in the fourth argument for the "women deacons" interpretation above (and will see in more detail below), the use of the term is best explained by Paul's (successful!) attempt to establish the qualifications for female deacons.

Finally, Schreiner says, "the lack of a possessive genitive with *gunaikos* does not rule out the possibility that these women are wives of deacons, since elsewhere in the New Testament the possessive genitives is not used when it is clearly the case that the women or men being described are wives and husbands (cf. Col 3:18–29; Eph 5:22–25; 1 Cor 7:2–4, 11, 14, 33; Matt 18:25; Mark 10:2)."[26] This is true, but this is not one of those cases where "it is clearly the case that the women or men being described are wives and husbands." That is partly what makes a "wives" rendering less probable.

Our brief examination of Schreiner's five "possible" problems with a "female-deacons" interpretation of 1 Tim 3:11 shows that they are not convincing. Indeed, one is better off following Schreiner's own personal conclusion: the text does speak of female deacons.

23. Schreiner, *RBMW*, 505, footnote 13.
24. Grudem, *Systematic Theology*, 919–20, footnote 25.
25. Cf. Doriani, *Women and Ministry*, 180–82.
26. Schreiner, *RBMW*, 505, footnote 13.

Confirming Argument B: 1 Timothy 3:11

KNIGHT'S EXEGESIS AND ITS PROBLEMS

In his commentary on the Pastoral Epistles, George Knight attempts to undercut arguments in favor of the "women-deacons" understanding of 1 Tim 3:11. But in an attempt to provide a sound exegesis, his arguments fare no better than those suggested by Schreiner. Knight says,

> Four positions have been taken: (1) The women are inherently part of the διάκονοι, (2) they are "deaconesses" distinguished from but comparable with the διάκονοι, (3) they are female assistants to the διάκονοι, or (4) they are the wives of the διάκονοι.[27]
>
> Those in verse eleven are too clearly and definitely distinguished from the διάκονοι (again by ὡσαύτως, the title διάκονοι, and the qualification μιᾶς γυναικὸς ἄνδρες for the διάκονοι) for (1) to be the meaning intended by Paul. (3) is preferable to (2) because the title διάκονοι is not used in v. 11 ... [28]

The fact that διάκονοι is not used in verse eleven means little unless we are already assuming that Paul is not talking about women deacons. If Paul *is* talking about women deacons and is distinguishing them and their requirements from male deacons in verses 8–10,[29] then it is possible that he isn't going to use the

---

27. Knight, *Pastoral Epistles*, 171. There is another possible interpretation beyond the ones listed, but must not be taken up here. Paul may be essentially talking about both the wives of deacons *who are deacons themselves*. That is, being a woman deacon and being a wife of a deacon are not mutually exclusive. Therefore, in this theology, qualified women may not be deacons unless they are the wives of male deacons. This would alleviate some of the tension between the two main interpretational options, though, as it will become apparent, it would not really alleviate any more exegetical difficulties than a "women deacons," interpretation. Nevertheless, this is a possibility rarely entertained by scholars and needs more exploration.

28. Ibid.

29. The NASB rendering captures well the tone of this contrast: "*These men* must also first be tested; *then let them serve* as deacons, if they are beyond reproach. *Women* must likewise be dignified, not malicious gossips, but temperate, faithful in all things" (emphasis mine).

exact same terms.[30] And since, as Köstenberger and Mounce pointed out, there was no feminine form of deacon, the only good option remaining was to use γυναῖκας. That is what the Apostle does. Thus, verse eight could be legitimately rendered "the *male* deacons" (because men are being talked about) and verse eleven rendered "the women *deacons*" (because there was no better alternative in saying what he is trying to say).

> (3) is preferable to (2) because the title διάκονοι is not used in verse eleven and seems to be used so self-consciously before and after verse eleven in unmistakable male categories (μιᾶς γυναικὸς ἄνδρες).[31]

Knight makes this same assertion later on: "Here it seems likely that the term is used in verse eleven in the same way that it is used in the immediately following verse, and as it was used in the preceding occurrence in verse two, i.e., as 'wife.'"[32] In both cases, the argument is essentially this: the same term is used before and after verse and is rendered 'wife,' so it should be rendered 'wife' in verse eleven.

But unless more contextual evidence is given, this assertion carries no weight. The very fact that the same word is used twice in a context does not in and of itself mean that the word must (or is even likely to) mean the same thing wherever it occurs in that textual vicinity. Careful exegesis often requires a case-by-case analysis to determine what's really going on (as exhausting as that is!).

And when one looks at each case, the differences between the use of γυνὴ in verses two and twelve in contrast to verse eleven are significant. Contextually, Paul seems to use ὡσαύτως ("likewise") in verse eleven in a way similar to its use in verse eight, indicating

---

30. This is not to say the term διάκονος is not sometimes associated with those who do preaching work; Paul refers to himself as a "servant" or "deacon" (διάκονος) along with Epaphras in Col 1:7, 23, 25. Acts 19:22 (and perhaps Col 4:7 and Eph 6:21). But, as we saw above, it is one thing for preachers to be helping and doing διάκονος-related work, and another for Scripture to make assertions about the nature and purpose of the diaconate via permanent qualifications, as in 1 Tim 3:1–13.

31. Knight, *Epistles*, 171.

32. Ibid.

Confirming Argument B: 1 Timothy 3:11

that the use of γυναικὸς in verse eleven is a categorical heading related to the chapter's broader discussion of church government. Thus, it signals an introduction to a specific group with specific qualifications,[33] though it may or may not[34] directly introduce a new, office of the church. This simply is not the case with the usage of γυνὴ in verses two and twelve.

Grammatically, in verses two and twelve, the term γυνὴ functions in the context of possession, ownership, or close relationship (and thus is genitive singular in each case) while in verse eleven the term is accusative plural, functioning as the subject of an infinitival clause governed by the verb δεῖ (v. 2) in a way that is closely parallel to "overseer" (v. 2) and "deacons" (v. 8). In all three cases, the qualifications for each category follow the accusative noun ("the overseer must be . . . ; likewise deacons must be . . . ; likewise the women must be . . . ").

Syntactically, the terms in verses two and twelve are in phrases included in lists of qualifications for offices, while in verse eleven the term is used to mark off the beginning of a set of qualifications for what appears to be an office or sub-office of the church itself. That is, verses two and twelve are making an assertion about the number of spouses an elder or deacon candidate must have (no more than one [μιᾶς]) or perhaps the quality of their marital status,[35] while verse eleven provides the qualifications for an entire subcategory (i.e., "deacons who are women") of an office itself.

---

33. Towner, *Letters to Timothy and Titus*, 266, footnote 28: "The adverb ὡσαύτως ('likewise'; 2:9; 3:8; Titus 2:3, 6) that changes the topic to 'women' serves to introduce a new but related case. As in the case of 'deacons,' in 3:8 (see discussion), the verb of necessity plus infinitive (δεῖ εἶναι) should be supplied from 3:2." Cf. Lewis, "The 'Women' of 1 Tim. 3:11," 167–75: "If γυναίκας were indeed the wives of deacons then in all probability καί, not ὡσαύτως, would have been used."

34. Thus, in the case of verse eight, it is used to introduce a new group that *is* a new office, while in verse eleven the term introduces a new group *within* that office—which is why verse eleven is part and parcel of the whole paragraph dealing with the diaconate.

35. *NET Bible* textual notes on 1 Tim 3:12 say "Or 'a man married only once' (similar NASB, NRSV, CEV), 'devoted solely to his wife' (cf. NLT; see 1 Tim 3:12; 4:9; Ti. 1:6). This phrase is often understood to refer to the marital

Thus, if γυνή in verse eleven was it is in verses two and twelve, Knight's argument based on the usage of the same word might be fair. Since this is not the case, and since there are significant differences in the usage of the term in verse eleven, Knight's conclusion that "(3) is preferable to (2)" is without warrant. Knight's argument that the term γυνή is used in "male categories" in verses two and twelve actually works against his position, since verse eleven is using the term in a different way. This makes verse eleven different, *not similar* to the way it is used in verses two and twelve, again favoring a rendering of "the women"/"women" (NASB, NRSV, NIV 2011, TNIV 2005, AMP, ASV, CEV, RSV, Barclay), "the women deacons" (NLT, footnote), "the women who are deacons" (TNIV 2001) or "women in this office" (REB) instead of a rendering of "their wives" (ESV, NET, NKJV, KJV, NIV 1984).

Knight says:

> γυνή both singular and plural, has the general meaning "woman/women," but is also often used to mean "wife/wives" (see BAGD). Both usages occur in the [Pauline Epistles] and especially in 1 Timothy ("woman" in 2:9, 10, 11, 12, 14; "wife in 3:2, 12; 5:9; cf. Ti. 1:6). Here it seems likely that the term is used in v.11 in the same way that it is used in the immediate following verse, and as it was used in the preceding occurrence in verse two, i.e., as "wife."[36]

Why does it "seem likely"? We're not told, and no clear reason is given.

Before stating his conclusion that the text should read "wives," Knight briefly summarizes the relevant usage of the term. But the specific information he provides doesn't favor one view or another. In fact, when one looks at *all* of the relevant data, the facts actually seem to favor the position he rejects.[37]

---

status of the church leader."

36. Knight, *Epistles*, 171.

37. The ESV and NRSV renders the term γυνη "woman" or "women," in the NT, Paul's writings, and Paul's letters to Timothy more than "wife" or "wives." So on this kind of general statistical basis, it is *unlikely*, not "likely" that it should be rendered "wives." Blackburn's detailed analysis also reveals

Confirming Argument B: 1 Timothy 3:11

After stating his deacons-wives conclusion, Knight makes a number of assertions (examined below). But, again, none of them favor "deacons wives":

> γυναῖκας is accusative because it, like Διακόνους in v.8, is governed by the understood δεῖ. With the bishop, and the deacons it is the role that gives warrant for the δεῖ εἶναι. Therefore, the γυναῖκας in v.11 are urged to manifest the four characteristics listed there, not because all women in the church must manifest these characteristics, but because of a special role that these "women" in particular have that demands these characteristics.[38]

At this point, virtually all can agree with what has been said. This isn't an argument in favor of either "deacons' wives" or "women deacons."

It is strange, then, that in the very next sentence Knight plainly says (in the form of an assumption) that these are deacons' wives, as if that assertion has somehow been established from what has just been said:

> *As spouses of the deacons* they are to be involved with their husbands as their husbands seek to fulfill their diaconal service. The translation "wives" expresses this unique relationship and responsibility.[39]

---

the same conclusion in, "Identity of 'the Women,'" 308-9: "Of some forty-six instances in which γυνή–γυναῖκες occurs after a reference to the husband(s), there are only four cases, all singular, where γυνή has no article or personal or reflexive pronoun (Mark 10:2; 12:19 (par. Luke 20:28); Luke 18:29; 1 Cor 7:11. Moreover, in each of these cases, unlike the situation in 1 Tim 3:11, γυνή is very closely related to the prior reference to the husband, either by the use of the correlatives ἀνήρ/ γυνή or by the wording that makes it absolutely certain that the γυνή is the wife of the man just mentioned. By contrast, in twenty-four of the remaining occurrences, γυνή is accompanied by both definite article and genitive personal (or reflexive) pronoun. The article without the pronoun appears in sixteen instances, but careful examination reveals that in almost every one of these occurrences γυνή is correlative with ἀνήρ (or designations for other family members, e.g., children, father, mother) or refers to a prior occurrence of γυνή *with* article and pronoun."

38. Knight, *Epistles*, 171.
39. Ibid., emphasis mine.

As it is apparent, Knight is arguing in a circle and/or begging the question: of course "the translation 'wives'" expresses the "unique relationship" of "spouses of the deacons," for one cannot be the spouse of a husband without being a wife! Again, nothing that is being said here substantiates the assertion that "wives" should be the translation of the women in 3:11. The only thing being said is that verse eleven should be translated "wives" because they are the spouses of their husbands—*but that is precisely the conclusion that is in question.* Why should γυναῖκας be rendered "wives" and understood as deacons' spouses? And why should 1 Tim 3:11 *not* be understood as referring to women deacons? Neither of these questions have been adequately answered. Nevertheless, Knight continues:

> Further, it is also more likely that Paul, who was wise concerning sexuality (cf., e.g., 2:9; 5:11, 15; and perhaps 5:6), would propose the deacons' wives as their assistants rather than women in general.[40]

Two responses may be offered to this argument. First, the argument once again assumes a conclusion without proving it: what reasons are given that the women in verse eleven are "assistants" at all? If these women in verse eleven are not assistants to deacons but are actually deacons themselves, the thrust of Knight's assertion about wisdom in sexuality is superfluous. Second, even if it is true that assistants are being talked about, (a) it has not been established that they are assistants specifically to the diaconate instead of to the church in general, and (b) it has not been established that assistantship requires them to be the wives of deacons. As an aside, it is noteworthy that the early church actually found female deacons (as opposed to deacons' wives) as a *deterrent* for sexual temptations, especially for baptisms.[41]

---

40. Ibid.

41. *Apostolic Constitutions*, 6.3.17, in *ANF*, 7:457, cited in Allison, *Historical Theology*, 595: "The deacon will anoint only their forehead with the holy oil; afterwards, the deaconess will anoint them. For there is no necessity that the women should be seen by the men. Only in the laying on of hands will the bishop anoint her head. After that, either you the bishop or a presbyter who is

Confirming Argument B: 1 Timothy 3:11

Knight next argues,

> Another consideration that favors the understanding "wives" in verse eleven is the omission of any reference to their marital status and fidelity (i.e., "the wife of one husband"), as is found with reference to the bishops and deacons (vv. 2, 12) and in the qualifications for enrollment for older widows (5:9). This omission is significant because this qualification is always mentioned in the [Pastoral Epistles] where positions of ministry or service are in view and because it stands out as such a striking difference between the otherwise nearly parallel qualifications of the διάκονοι and the γυναῖκας.[42]

The "always mentioned" in the Pauline Epistles that Knight is talking about, outside 1 Tim 3, is only *one verse* (Tim 1:6)! And in that verse it's talking about (male) elders, not deacons of any kind. It is no wonder that Knight gives no references or citations for this assertion—it is not as significant as he makes it sound.[43]

His second reason for believing the omission of marital status is significant is "because it stands out as such a striking difference between the otherwise nearly parallel qualifications of the διάκονοι and the γυναῖκας. The omission can, however, be explained if the requirement is inherent in their position as wives of διάκονοι." Is Knight really suggesting that in the first century church women having multiple husbands was just as big of a problem as men having multiple wives? There is simply no basis for such an assertion—as if female polygamy were so obviously important that Paul had to include it in the list of qualifications for female deacons.

---

under you will, according to the solemn rite, name over them the Father, Son, and Holy Spirit, and then dip them in the water. Then let a deacon receive the man [who has] been baptized and a deaconess receive the woman. In this way, the conferring of this unbreakable seal will take place with a proper decency."

42. Knight, *Epistles*, 171.

43. Wallace and Burer made the same kind of error regarding Rom 16:7 (see Bauckham, *Gospel Women*, 174), and several more of these kinds of misleading arguments by Knight have been documented in Payne, *Man and Woman*, 277–380.

A Case for Female Deacons

Perhaps Paul is not talking about the number of spouses when he gives the qualification, but rather about marital status and devotion to one's spouse, as he does elsewhere for men (1 Tim 3) and women (1 Tim 5:9). In that case, it is quite reasonable that Paul omits the qualification because he is assuming (1) that these women are married (though not necessarily married to a deacon), or (2) they are unmarried[44] either due either to devotion to ministry (perhaps in the same sense as Phoebe, a διάκονον, in Rom 16:1, assuming she was single) or because they are widows (cf. 1 Tim 5:9), or for some other reason. But the answer "because they are deacons' wives" is certainly not the only option, nor the most plausible.

But if the "women deacons" position is challenged by the omission of a marital qualification, the "deacon's wives" position has an omissions problem of its own. As we have seen previously, the question is not merely why there is an omission of "the wife of one husband." A bigger question, if 3:11 is really talking about deacons' wives, is why there is an omission of (a) qualifications for *elders'* wives in 3:1–7, and (b) a pronoun, article, or some other indicator actually stating that these women are in a relationship with male deacons. As Towner summarized, "if 'wives of deacons' was meant, it would have been more common to indicate this with either a possessive pronoun [e.g., γυναῖκας ὑμῶν, "your wives," or "their wives"] or the definite article (e.g., 1 Cor 7:2, 3; Eph 5:22; Col 3:18, 24; 1 Pet 3:1)."[45]

Knight says,

> Furthermore, this understanding of γυναῖκας as "wives" also provides the solution for the reference to γυναῖκας at

---

44. Lewis, "Women of 1 Tim 3:11," 173: "The backdrop of 1 Tim seems to indicate that women were having difficulty fulfilling their womanly responsibilities especially to the home. If the women of verse eleven could be married, surely a great deal of restrictive legislation concerning the home needed to be spelled out. If anywhere, Paul needed to say "women likewise" after 1 Tim 3:12. Yet he is instead strangely silent. It is for [this reason] that it is suggested that γυναῖκας be restricted to women who are unmarried. The fact that these women had no family responsibilities enabled them to give their undivided attention to the church." Cf. Lenski, *Interpretation of St. Paul's Epistles*, 599.

45. Towner, *Letters to Timothy and Titus*, 266, footnote 28.

Confirming Argument B: 1 Timothy 3:11

this place in the pericope. If it is wives that are in view, then the verse fits here as another qualification necessary for one who would be a deacon and who would conduct his ministry with his wife's assistance. Thus the wife's qualifications are part and parcel of his qualifications for the office of διάκονος. And after giving the qualifications for the deacon's wife, Paul then goes on to the deacon's fidelity to his wife and his children and thereby completes the picture of his family life (v.12).[46]

Certainly elders' wives have just as much (or more) to contribute to their husbands' work as deacons' wives. We have no mention of elders' wives. And, what if a deacons' wife has a number of children and helps run a family business and the deacon in question simply doesn't want his wife to leave her primary duties at home to help with additional work at church? Certainly if wives are in view, Paul is requiring a sacrifice of time that could profoundly affect the dynamic of the household (and this would potentially contradict Paul's admonition that deacons should "manage their children and their own households well" in verse twelve).

Furthermore, what if the wife of the deacon is not a Christian? We know the Corinthians struggled with "mixed" marriages (1 Cor 7), and there is no reason to think that problem is only local. We can assume the "women" in 1 Tim 3:11 are Christians if they are female deacons, but is the same assumption required if the women are simply the wives of deacons?

It makes better sense to believe that Paul is describing women deacons. In doing so, he is providing qualifications for them in way that does not (a) exclude them from the same office that male deacons work in, or (b) sacrifice their distinct female identity, or (c) create an entirely new, third church office ("deaconess") apart from the office of deacon.[47] Paul includes a discussion of women

---

46. Knight, *Epistles*, 172.

47. Indeed, as Lewis, "Women of 1 Tim. 3:11," 171, remarked, "It would seem strange for Paul to introduce a third office of the church so briefly and then return to the former topic of male deacons without some further explanation." Contrast with MacArthur, *John MacArthur Study Bible*, 1835. Cf. Doriani, *Women and Ministry*, 181–82; Hurley, *Man and Woman*, 232.

43

deacons in the very center of the most explicit text on the qualifications for deacons in the Scriptures and lists essentially the same qualifications (because the office is the same) though with slight differences (because gender determines the particular challenges they face in the assuming of that office).[48]

Indeed, if γυναῖκας is used to refer to women deacons, why would we not expect it to be in a discussion about the offices of the church?[49] *Where else* in the pericope (or Scripture, for that matter) would Knight place the discussion of women deacons? As we have seen time and again, a "women deacons" translation is less troublesome than a "deacons' wives" translation.[50]

Knight goes on to deal with the lack of the definite article in 1 Tim 3:11:

> It has been objected to this understanding of γυναῖκες that no indication of relationship is found in the text, not even a definite article before γυναῖκας. It may be responded that in the whole pericope Paul refers to people anarthrously (Διακόνους, v.8; διάκονοι, v.12; τέκνων, v.12; τέκνα, v.3; γυναικὸς as "wife," v.12 as in v.2, in both cases

---

48. Dibelius and Conzelmann's position is similar, but more structured. They say that verses 8–10 applies to deacons of both genders while v.11 refers specifically to female deacons and verses 12–13 refers to male deacons (see their work "The Pastoral Epistles," 58). This would alleviate the "placement" of verse eleven in the text, and the problem of the placement of verse ten, which is unique to the entire discussion in 1 Tim 3:1–13 (see footnote below on verses 10–11).

49. Blackburn, "Identity," 307: "Roloff has observed astutely that the position of verse eleven can be used *against* the notion that deacons wives are under consideration. Had they been, would not such a reference be more natural *after* verse twelve, with its requirement concerning the deacon's marriage?"

50. As mentioned before, there may be a possible contrast drawn between verse ten and verse eleven which is more visible in the NASB: "*These men* must also first be tested; *then let them serve* as deacons, if they are beyond reproach. *Women* must likewise be dignified, not malicious gossips, but temperate, faithful in all things" (emphasis mine), and presumably, "then let them serve." This seems consistent with Paul's train of thought. Furthermore, verse ten in combination with verse twelve presents a problem (namely, verse ten seems to be conclusive to verses 8–9, which makes verse twelve appear out of place, regardless if verse eleven is in the text or not) that may contribute to explaining why the paragraph flows as it does.

Confirming Argument B: 1 Timothy 3:11

preceding anarthrous words, ἄνδρες in v.12, ἄνδρα in v.2; τὸν ἐπίσκοπον, v.2 is the sole exception, probably because of its generic usage). If verse eleven had been written after verse twelve, the understanding of the γυναῖκες as wives, even without any qualification, would likely be more apparent just because of the order and the usage of the anarthrous γυναικός, which would have been immediately preceding. However, the effect of verse twelve on our understanding of verse eleven still remains, even with the order of the verses as we have them.[51]

Knight's first assertion is that since Paul generally does not use the article for people in 1 Tim 3, it may not be justified to expect an article for γυναῖκας in verse eleven. This is possible, but it fails to address why a *possessive pronoun* (e.g., "their wives") or another word arrangement ("deacons' wives") is not used to identify the relationship of the women. Additionally, the anarthrous words cited have no reference to these people's relationships with others, whereas here a relationship is being posited. So an argument for anarthrous nouns *in general* doesn't truly address the unique situation being proposed for verse eleven. In fact, the very absence of the article may put these women in a similar position to the others—they are a special category of people that Paul is referring to.

Knight's second assertion is purely theoretical: "If verse eleven had been written after verse twelve . . . " But since verse eleven does *not* come after verse twelve, little is proved. This is conceded, in effect, when we read, "However, the effect of verse twelve on our understanding of verse eleven still remains, even with the order of the verses as we have them."

In conclusion, R. Lewis was correct in saying, "To infuse a marital unity between verses 8–10 and verse eleven seems beyond the text. There simply is no such connection."[52] H. Kent also concludes that without some better indicator of the relationship

---

51. Knight, *Epistles*, 172.
52. Lewis, "Women of 1 Tim. 3:11," 169.

intended, "the reader is left to infer 'women deacons.'"[53] And that is where we are left.

DANIEL WALLACE ON 1 TIMOTHY 3:11

In his essay entitled "May Women Be Deacons? A Prelude to Dialogue,"[54] Greek scholar Daniel Wallace makes a concise argument against women deacons that, for the most part, resembles the common objections that we have already observed above. Below is a brief refutation on some of Wallace's major points.[55] I apologize for the repetition, but it helps in demonstrating the popularity of certain errors.

> In response are five arguments: (1) If women deacons are in view in verse eleven, it seems rather strange that they should be discussed right in the middle of the qualifications for male deacons, rather than by themselves.

As shown above, this argument actually supports (not undermines) a female deacons interpretation. The placement of 3:11, as Wallace says, is indeed odd. But "women deacons" explains this oddity the best.

> (2) Paul indeed seems to go out of his way to indicate that women are NOT deacons in the very next verse, for he says "Deacons must be husbands of one wife";

That isn't true if Paul is resuming his discussion on male deacons from verses 8–10. Wallace is also making the half-hearted assertion that we saw from Grudem above: "husbands" works against women deacons (because husbands are male), yet at the same time, "husbands" *doesn't* work against deacons (because we realize church officers aren't actually required to be married or have kids). Again, elders do not have to have wives or children any

---

53. Kent, "Pastoral Epistles," 141.
54. Wallace, "May Women Be Deacons?"
55. Wallace has elsewhere been shown to be imbalanced in his exegesis of female-related texts. See Richard Bauckham, *Gospel Women*, 172–80; Epp, *Junia*, 72–120; Belleville, "Iounian," 231–49.

Confirming Argument B: 1 Timothy 3:11

more than deacons have to be husbands or men. Why then does Paul include marital and family qualifications? Precisely because the vast majority of first century candidates for elders or deacons were married and had kids; we must allow the human authors of divine Scripture to make ordinary assumptions.

> (3) as to why he didn't mention wives in the section on elders, there are one of two possibilities that come to mind: (a) since Paul was addressing some real problems in Ephesus, it may well be that the deacons' wives had been a major concern; (b) concomitantly, since deacons' duties involved taking care of physical needs, they would have been in control of the mercy funds in the church—and, if so, it would be imperative for their wives to be 'dignified, not scandalmongers, but sober, and trustworthy in everything' (REB). One can readily see the psychological realities of such instructions to deacons' wives: they must be tight-lipped when it came to discussing the very personal needs of the body.

These two explanations are not compelling, and they are on-par with Knight's exegetical evaluations: the arguments can be used to favor women deacons just as much as deacons' wives.

In (a), text is over-contextualized. Wallace is essentially saying, "this is a special case for Ephesus, so unless the elders of the church Paul was writing to had the same problem, we shouldn't expect Paul to list qualifications for elders' wives." But, what *isn't* a special case? Do not *all* of Paul's epistles to churches address situation-specific problems in those churches? Couldn't we say that *everything Paul mentions* in 1 Timothy is a major concern for him, which is why he includes it in the small letter? If so, then this argument isn't saying much. Furthermore, a person making a case for women deacons could make the same argument: Paul was addressing some unique problems in Ephesus, and it may well be that the qualifications for men and women in the office of deacon were the unique problems.

In (b) we encounter another argument that can be used to favor women deacons. Would it not be imperative for women deacons—those who take care of physical needs and finances—to be "dignified, not scandalmongers, but sober, and trustworthy in everything"? Wallace says "One can readily see the psychological realities of such instructions to deacons' wives: they must be tight-lipped when it came to discussing the very personal needs of the body." How would that *not* also apply to women deacons? Wallace continues:

> (4) Again, if verse eleven is addressed to women deacons, why are most of the qualifications not listed—that is, the only qualifications that pertain to the women would be the four items listed in this verse. But would they be allowed to be addicted to strong drink?

The difference in alcohol prohibition is probably due to the fact that, generally speaking, men have (and had) the biggest problem with alcohol. But the absence of specific commands to specific grounds doesn't mean they are exempt from the commands. Is Wallace suggesting that because only women are specifically scolded for gossip (1 Tim 5:13), that men are allowed to gossip? Of course not. Paul doesn't have to repeat all the instruction of godliness for men for women, and vice versa. The point of the distinctions (which are very minor) is probably to highlight (either as a general rule or for the particular situation at the time) the particular challenges that come with being a man or a woman in the particular office of deacon.

> The very fact that all these requirements seem so universal and yet are given specifically only to the men seems to argue against women deacons being in view in verse eleven.

This simply is not the case. The requirements outline the more specific qualifications for each sex. And just because Paul singles out men or women does not mean that instruction is only limited to them as men or women,[56] but simply that such specific instruction is *especially applicable to them* as either a man or a woman. If Wallace were consistent in this kind of hermeneutic throughout

---

56. A great case study is Col 3:20–21. See Moo, *Letters to the Colossians*, 306.

Confirming Argument B: 1 Timothy 3:11

Scripture, we would have to admit that women should be allowed to covet their neighbor's husband, since the Ten Commandments only say "you shall not covet your neighbor's wife" (Exod 20:17) and not "or your neighbor's husband."

> (5) Finally, the original manuscripts of the New Testament were not divided by chapters and verses. And sometimes our divisions get in the way of seeing the overall context. There seems to be an unnatural break between chapters 2 and 3—or, at least, one that is too abrupt. I take it that 2:8 through 3:16 are all addressing conduct in the church. The issues revolve around men and women throughout these two chapters. And the very fact that Paul says in 2:12 that women were not to teach or exercise authority over men seems to govern what he says in chapter 3 as well. Thus, if deacons are in a role of exercising authority, then I would argue that Paul implicitly restricts such a role to men.

However, recognizing the tight relation between chapters one and two of 1 Timothy actually supports a "women deacons" interpretation rather than undermining it. In the conclusion to his thorough essay, Perry says:

> While Paul's use of γυνή in 3:12 has led some commentators to translate γυναίκας as "wives" in 3:11, the transition from 3:11 to 3:12 is explained better by the remarkable omission of "μιας γυναικός άνδρα" in 3:8–10. Paul omits the "one-woman-man" policy in 3:8–10 because he is referring there to character requirements for both male and female diaconal candidates. He makes this point explicit in 3:11 by repeating the character qualities of 3:8–10 for those candidates who are "women." In 3:12, for those candidates who are men, he underscores their fidelity to "one woman" (μιας γυναικός ανδρες; 3:12) even as he calls women to be "faithful in all things" (πίστας εν πάσιν), including their marriages, in 3:11 (cf. ενός ανδρός γυνή in 5:9). In 3:13, Paul again addresses the general group of candidates for diaconal leadership, both men and women, to encourage them about the benefits of their ministry both for their personal faith and for

their public standing. Based on Paul's alternating pattern of addressing "men" then "women" in 1 Tim. 2, the clear syntactical parallel between 2:9 and 3:11 (ὡσαύτως γυναῖκας and γυναῖκας ὡσαύτως), the coherence of the whole and tight framing of 3:11 within the discussion about "deacons" (3:8–13), I conclude that the "women" Paul describes in 3:11 are women candidates for diaconal service or "women deacons."[57]

We might also add that merely "exercising authority" (something women do over their children and even over their husbands,[58] for example) neither directly prohibits women from anything, nor puts women in the category of 1 Tim 2:12.

CONCLUSION

The most basic aspects of exegesis—context, syntax, structure—point to a "women deacons" interpretation of 1 Tim 3:11. Objections to this position are not persuasive. In fact, many of the opposing arguments have been found to be self-refuting and inadvertently supportive of a "women deacons" interpretation. This conclusion finds a home with some of the most respected reformed and evangelical exegetical scholars of our day, and legitimately so. In the next chapter, we will shift gears and look at the historical legitimacy of female deacons.

---

57. See Perry, "Phoebe of Cenchreae," 32–33. Be sure to see his whole essay for more on this particular argument.

58. 1 Cor 7:4.

5

Confirming Argument C: Historical Theology

> C. Female deacons ("deaconesses") are not foreign to the historical church. Rather, female deacons have been conceptually approved by Christian leaders and have actually existed in many churches throughout history.

INTRODUCTION: HISTORICAL METHODOLOGY

Church history is greatly diverse. But it can be a wonderful guide to prevent the church from slipping into error. Given today's vast written sources, we may readily learn from others' ministries and from others' mistakes.

The argument for the validity of women deacons would be particularly open to question if there were no female deacons in the history of the church. The argument would be further weakened if the church continually saw female deacons as a serious threat and continually argued against the doctrine. Conversely, the existence of female deacons in the history of the church lends a measure of support for the validity of the practice. The support is strengthened if female deacons served in the same general sense of male deacons (i.e., in a church-recognized position) and if they existed in most eras of church history. As it will be demonstrated, these latter two options are precisely the case.

51

It should be noted, however, that the existence of female deacons in church history is not meant to imply that there have not been many places and times in church history in which female deacons were *not* recognized or utilized. No doubt, for many examples given below, a counter-example could be given to demonstrate that women deacons were not recognized in certain churches (this is especially true when comparing the Western and Eastern branches of the church). So I am not suggesting that female deacons were *always* the norm or are even that the majority of historical witnesses and churches always supported them. Rather, the chapter merely seeks to establish what the premise says: *female deacons ("deaconesses") are not foreign to the historical church. Rather, female deacons have been conceptually approved by Christian leaders and have actually existed in many churches throughout history.*

The distinction between conceptual approval and actual existence primarily acknowledges that in many cases Christians have believed female deacons are legitimate even where they did not exist in churches during their time. This is true even today. There are many churches whose leaders believe female deacons are legitimate, yet none serve in their churches for one reason or another (e.g., "let's not rock the boat by giving her the title"). This distinction also shows that for female deacons that *do* exist in churches, this also establishes their acceptance in the theology of the church. In other words, while it is possible to have Christians *believing* that female deacons are legitimate while not *having* female deacons in the church, it is not possible to have female deacons in the church without Christians believing that female deacons are legitimate.

One should also not overlook the importance of historical situations where Christians have approved of female deacons but have none serving in their churches. In fact, it could be argued that such cases should be given more weight when compared to situations with extant deaconesses because it suggests that such Christians are willing to affirm female deacons even when the idea may not be popular or accepted. Take John Calvin, for example, who acknowledged the legitimacy of female deacons when most churches during his day did not accept them. As with many of

CONFIRMING ARGUMENT C: HISTORICAL THEOLOGY

Calvin's theological positions, his convictions stemmed from Scripture—such is the essence of the Protestant call of *sola scriptura*. This demonstrates that members of the church find female deaconesses supported by the Scriptures even if they are denied by contemporary church tradition.

Having outlined a few key points of our methodology, let us begin. Our survey is primarily chronological and is largely indebted to J. Olson's seminal work entitled *Deacons and Deaconesses Through the Centuries* (1992, revised 2005). The section on the Medieval Church gleans heavily from V. Karras's 2004 essay, "Female Deacons in the Byzantine Church," which is based on her doctoral dissertation of 2002.[1]

APOSTLES TO AUGUSTINE

The office of deacon underwent considerable evolution during the first four Christian centuries. The concept of the female deacon was often obscured with other terms such as "widow," "virgin," and "abbess" (head of a female monastery) sometimes representing formal positions (e.g., "ordained"), sometimes not ("appointed" and not "ordained"). Thus, in the fourth century there was the "widow-deaconess," the "virgin-deaconess," and other such variations.[2] When combined with the numerous other ecclesiastical roles such as "subdeacon," "archdeacon," "gatekeeper," "singer," and "reader," the historical narrative of the origins of the various offices and their meanings in various contexts, as these related to the office of deacon, can become quite dizzying.

One general observation is that within the first several centuries of the church, the female deacon branch of the diaconate spawned its own office of "deaconess," and this often had specific functions that differed from those of male deacons. In many cases, women deaconesses were subordinate to male deacons, though

---

1. Her work is particularly insightful as it refutes many of the anti-deaconess claims made in A. G. Martimort's *Deaconesses: A Historical Study*, which is also a standard work in this area of historical theology.

2. Olson, *Deacons and Deaconesses*, 53–55.

"deaconess" was still considered an office (often ordained). Whatever the case, we shall try to stay focused on the reality of female deacons serving in church-recognized positions comparable to male deacons in the historic church and avoid a detailed discussion of the development of church offices.

Around the year 112 C.E., the Roman administrator Pliny the Younger of Bithynia wrote a letter to the emperor Trajan, saying that he (Pliny) had tortured "two maidservants who were called deaconesses [*ministrae*]."[3] Little can be extrapolated from this reference since it is only in passing. Scholars have pointed that it is not always necessary to translate the Latin term *ministrae* as "deaconess" in female contexts such as these, especially since it is uncertain how much Pliny knew of the particular ecclesiastical functions of these women. So it is wise not to put too much weight on this reference. Nevertheless, this could be the earliest reference to female deacons outside biblical documents.

The second notable item is from Clement of Alexandria (c. 150–215), who confirms the interpretation of 1 Tim 3:11 espoused in this work: "For we know what the honorable Paul in one of his letters to Timothy prescribed regarding women deacons."[4] This is important to note since there are few direct references to 1 Tim 3:11 in early church documents. This rare reference corroborates our interpretation that the verse deals with women deacons, and not just deacons' wives, and confirms that this interpretation was held as early as the second century AD.

The anonymous *Didascalia Apostolorum* (early 200s) gives insight into the practice of the Syrian Christian church. The author discusses deaconesses at length. Two major quotes shall suffice to demonstrate:

> Therefore O Bishop appoint for thyself workers of righteousness and helpers to help with thee to life, electing those who please thee from all the people (S. and appoint

---

3. Pliny, *Epistle* X, 96.8, cited in Olson, *Deacons and Deaconesses*, 29. Cf. English renderings of *diakonos* as "minister" in Col 1:7, 25; 2 Cor 3:6; Eph 3:7.

4. Clement of Alexandria, *Stromateis* 3.6.53, cited in Liefield, *Discovering Biblical Equality*, 122.

Deacons). The man who is elected is for many oversights that are required, but a woman for the service of the women, for there are houses where thou canst not send a Deacon to the women on account of the heathen. Send a Deaconess for many things. The office of a woman Deaconess is required, first, when women go down to the water it is necessary that they be anointed by a Deaconess, and it is not fitting that the anointing oil should be given to a woman to touch; but rather the Deaconess. For it is necessary for the Priest who baptizeth to anoint her who is baptized; but when there is a woman, and especially a Deaconess, it is not fitting for the women that they be seen by the men but that by the laying on of the hand the head alone be anointed as of old time the Priests and Kings of Israel were anointed. Thou also, in like manner, by laying on thy hand anoint the head of those who receive baptism, whether of men or of women, and afterwards, whether thou thyself baptize or command the Deacon or the Elder to baptize, let it be a Deaconess as we said before, who anoints the women. Let a man repeat over them the names of the invocation of the Godhead in the water. And when she that is baptized arises from the water, let the Deaconess receive her, and teach her and educate her, in order that the unbreakable seal of baptism be with purity and holiness. Therefore we affirm that the service of a woman, a Deaconess, is necessary and obligatory, because even our Lord and Saviour was served by the hand of women deaconesses, who were Mary the Magdalene and Mary (Cod. S. daughter) of James, the mother of Joses, and the mother of Zebedee's children, with other women. This service of Deaconesses is necessary also to thee for many things, for in the houses of the heathen where there are believing women, a Deaconess is required that she may go in and visit those who are sick and serve them with whatever they need and anoint [S. wash] those who are healed from sicknesses.[5]

---

5. *Didascalia Apostolorum* XVI, "Of the appointment of Deacons and Deaconesses," in Gibson, *The Didascalia apostolorum* in English, 78. The "S." notations indicate literal translations from the Syriac version.

A Case for Female Deacons

In an earlier statement the same document highlights the honor associated with both male and female deacons:

> But the deacon stands in the place of Christ, and you should love him. The deaconess, however, shall be honored by you in place of the Holy Spirit.[6]

Canon nineteen of the ecumenical Council of Nicaea (325) contains the following instruction regarding deaconesses:

> Concerning the Paulianists who have flown for refuge to the Catholic Church, it has been decreed that they must by all means be rebaptized; and if any of them who in past time have been numbered among their clergy should be found blameless and without reproach, let them be rebaptized and ordained by the Bishop of the Catholic Church; but if the examination should discover them to be unfit, they ought to be deposed. Likewise in the case of their deaconesses, and generally in the case of those who have been enrolled among their clergy, let the same form be observed. And we mean by deaconesses such as have assumed the habit, but who, since they have no imposition of hands, are to be numbered only among the laity.

There are various interpretations of this canon due to the ambiguity of whether or not some deaconesses were especially ordained by the "imposition of hands." Karras contends that the passage indicates that the ordination of deaconesses was not foreign to the fourth century church:

> ... the fact that deaconesses were singled out for special mention precisely because they had not been ordained makes it clear that there was a difference in practice here between the two churches; that is, either the Paulianists or the catholic Church considered deaconesses a nonclerical order and hence did not confer ordination on them. If both churches had viewed them as nonclergy, there would have been no reason to mention them at all.

---

6. *Didascalia Apostolorum* 9.1, cited in Olson, *Deacons and Deaconesses*, 41.

> Furthermore, if it were the Catholic Church that did not ordain deaconesses or consider them to be clergy, there would have been no reason to mention them since the required re-ordination for Paulianist clergy would have been impossible in the case of the deaconess; everyone would already know that they had lay status. The logical inference, then, is that the canon excluded Paulianist deaconesses from the re-ordination possible for other orders because, since they were not ordained in the Paulianist Church, they were considered laypersons, not ordained clergy, even in the heretical church. In other words, the purpose of this canon, as with many of those dealing with the Montanist Church in North Africa, was to try as much as possible to integrate heretical clergy into the catholic clergy so that they could remain with their communities; in the case of deaconesses, however, while it was possible for them to continue their ministry, it was impossible to consider their ministry to be a clerical one, as in the catholic Church, since the Paulianist deaconesses were not ordained clergy.[7]

In any case, women deacons, whether they were ordained or non-ordained, were apparently integral to imperial Christianity.

The *Apostolic Constitutions* (375–80), which also contains an edited version of the *Didascalia Aposolorum*, are comprised of eight books of church order and instruction that harmonize with similar documents of the same period:

> Dip them [baptismal candidates] in the water; and let a deacon receive the man, and a deaconess the woman, so that the conferring of this inviolable seal may take place with a becoming decency.[8]
>
> Let the porters stand at the entries of the men, and observe them. Let the deaconesses also stand at those of the women, like shipmen. For the same description and

---

7. Karras, "Female Deacons," 272–89.

8. *Apostolic Constitutions*, 6.3.17, in ANF, 7:457, cited in Allison, *Historical Theology*, 595, and also in Olson, *Deacons and Deaconesses*, 57.

pattern was both in the tabernacle of the testimony and in the temple of God.[9]

The ordination prayer for deaconesses in the same document says,

> O Eternal God, the Father of our Lord Jesus Christ, the creator of man and of woman, who didst replenish with the Spirit Miriam, and Deborah, and Anna, and Huldah; who didst not disdain that Thy only begotten Son should be born of a woman; who also in the tabernacle of the testimony, and in the temple, didst ordain women to be keepers of Thy holy gates,[10] do Thou now also look down upon this Thy servant, who is to be ordained to the office of a deaconess.[11]

As dealt with in the *Apostolic Constitutions*, it is clear that the deaconess played a critical role in the life of the church: "Let not any woman address herself to the deacon or bishop without the deaconess."[12]

Olson believes that the *Apostolic Constitutions* show evidence of the beginnings of subordination of deaconesses to deacons:

> Some of the responsibilities that the *Apostolic Constitutions* did not give to the widows went to the deaconesses, but the *Apostolic Constitutions* also made deaconesses dependent on deacons in a growing hierarchy of church office. The edited version of the *Didascalia* in the *Apostolic Constitutions* added passages that refer to the deaconess as subordinate to the deacon: Let the deaconess "not do or say anything without the deacon."[13]

---

9. *Apostolic Constitutions*, 2.57. The reference of the women at the entrance of the tent of meeting can be found in Exod 38:8, 1 Sam 2:22, and Ezek 8:14.

10. The reference here is to 1 Sam 2:22; Exod 38:8; Judg 5:24.

11. *Apostolic Constitutions*, 8.20.

12. Ibid., 2.26.

13. Olson, *Deacons and Deaconesses*, 60, quoting from *Apostolic Constitutions*, 2:26.

Confirming Argument C: Historical Theology

Nevertheless, the ordination of women deacons (deaconesses) was more or less common from the time of Nicaea onward, especially in Eastern churches.[14]

While some women avoided deaconess ordination for various reasons,[15] others thrived and had an enormous impact on the church. Two examples include Olympias (born in the 360s and friend of John Chrysostom) and Melania the Younger (383–439, friend of Augustine).

When she was twenty-five, Olympias lost her husband after being married for only two years. She then "devoted her life and wealth to the church. She was an ordained a deaconess [by the bishop of Constantinople (Nectatius)] when she was about 30 years of age."[16] She supported the church, built hospitals, gave "land and money, cared for the sick, and corresponded with Chrysostom while he was in exile."[17] Her successor was Elisanthia.[18]

Melania (Melanie) has a similar story of tragedy followed by a life given to the ministry. After the death of her two children, she went to Africa and later to Jerusalem where she founded a monastery that essentially trained women for service as deaconesses. Augustine personally "advised them [Melanie and Pinian, another friend] not just to found a monastery but to 'give both a house and an income to each monastery' so that it could survive."[19]

A few years after Augustine became bishop of Hippo, Olympias launched a convent of her own where see was Abbess. The monastery, named *Olympiados*, was primarily designed to house female deacons and virgins, and as "many as 250 women lived there."[20] The monastery was at one point disbanded because of

---

14. Karras, "Female Deacons," 273: "The evidence for ordained female deacons in the early Church period, at least in portions of the Eastern Church, is clear and unambiguous."
15. See Olson, *Deacons and Deaconesses*, 62.
16. Ibid.
17. Ibid.
18. See Karras, "Female Deacons," 282.
19. Ranft, *Women and the Religious Life*, 12.
20. Olson, *Deacons and Deaconesses*, 89. Schaff noted in *History of the*

Olympias's association with Chrysostom—who had been exiled due to conflict with the imperial party. By providence, she saw the rebuilding of the monastery before her death at age forty-seven.

In later centuries, the Western church seems to have cooled to the idea of women deacons—or at least their ordination.[21] Canon twenty-six of the Council of Orange (441) declared, "Let no one proceed to the ordination of deaconesses anymore."[22] Canon twenty-one of the Council of Epaon (517) declared, "We abrogate completely, in the entire kingdom, the consecration of widows who are named deaconesses."[23] Finally, the Council of Orleans (533) decreed that, "No longer shall the blessing of women deaconesses be given because of the weakness of the sex."[24] Although the "blessing" here may primarily refer only to ordination, it is clear that the edict was seeking to end a practice previously upheld by the church. Indeed, the decree demonstrates the growing tension, by the fifth and sixth centuries, between church preference and earlier church practice with regard to the ordination of deaconesses.

Christian Church 2:399: "It should not be forgotten that many virgins of the early church devoted their whole energies as deaconesses to the care of the sick and the poor, or exhibited as martyrs a degree of passive virtue and moral heroism altogether unknown before."

21. Buchheimer, "History of the Female Diaconate," 276–83: "It may be well to note that the female diaconate was never forbidden by any Eastern council, nor, with the exception of a few local synods in Gaul, was it ever abolished by the Western Church. Gradually however, the office fell into disuse, and the deaconess passed out of sight. This was, no doubt, due to the rise and spread of false ascetic principles, and in particular to the practice of religious celibacy. The deaconess was placed under the pernicious vow of celibacy and became a nun."

22. Cited in Swidler, *Jesus Was a Feminist*, 223.

23. Ibid.

24. Cited in Olson, *Deacons and Deaconesses*, 61. Buchheimer, "History of the Female Diaconate," 278, notes that "In spite of these prohibitions the female diaconate maintained its existence in Gaul for over 100 years."

CONFIRMING ARGUMENT C: HISTORICAL THEOLOGY

FROM AUGUSTINE TO WYCLIF

Female deacons in the medieval church were far less prominent than in the early church. This is true for at least three reasons that can only be broadly summarized here. First, the increase in the practice of infant baptism reduced the need for deaconesses (deaconesses, recall, were needed to baptize unclothed adult women).[25] Second, the imperial church moved female deacons into a more non-ordained, monastic role (abbess-deaconess). Third, the office of deacon quickly evolved into "a stepping-stone to priesthood," and since the priesthood was generally restricted to men, it would have been odd and awkward for women to try to enter the office of deaconess.

The ordination of women deacons was practiced in the early to mid-medieval period, but began to wane around the time of the crusades. This was especially true for the Eastern Church (Byzantine). Qualifications for female deaconess were even given (strict) regulations at the great ecumenical Council of Chalcedon (451):

> A woman shall not receive the laying on of hands as a deaconess under forty years of age, and then only after searching examination. And if, after she has had hands laid on her and has continued for a time to minister, she shall despise the grace of God and give herself in marriage, she shall be anathematized and the man united to her.[26]

This age requirement was actually "twenty years younger than the emperor Theodosius had required sixty years earlier."[27] Other

25. See Grosdidier de Matons, "La femme dans l'empire byzantin," 40; cited in Karras, "Female Deacons," 277.

26. Canon 15, in *NPNF*, 14:279.

27. Pitra, *Iuris ecclesiastici Graecorum historia et monumenta iussu Pit ix. Pont. Max.*, 1:528; cited in Karras, "Female Deacons," 275. Schaff provides his own account in *History of the Christian Church*, 2:260: "The office of deaconess, which, under the strict separation of the sexes in ancient times, and especially in Greece, was necessary to the completion of the diaconate, and which originated in the apostolic ... continued in the Eastern church down to the twelfth century ... Formerly, from regard to the apostolic precept in 1 Tim 5:9, the deaconesses were required to be sixty years of age. The general council of Chalcedon, however, in 451, reduced the canonical age to forty years." Schaff

than the fact that this is an ecumenical council, it is important to note that not only does the church recognize female deacons, but also that the "laying on of hands" is assumed.[28]

In Justinian's Novel 3 (500s), female deacons are clearly listed among the clergy:[29]

> Since the novel limits presbyters to 60, male deacons to 100, female deacons to 40, subdeacons to 90, readers to 110, and chanters to 25, it is clear that female deacons are included among the "most reverend clergy" totaling 425 persons. This novel was reiterated in the *Basilics* III, 2, 1.[30]

In the ordination rites of the Barberini *Euchologion* (700s), deacon and deaconesses, along with archdeacons, presbyters, and bishops, were ranked among the "major orders" of the clergy.[31] The

---

cites Rom 16:1–2 and his first volume church history as evidence for women deacons in the apostolic age.

28. Throughout this period in church history the requirements for female deacons were often more strict than for male deacons. In the case of the Byzantine church, "The requirements for entry to the female diaconate were far more restrictive than for the male diaconate, even in late antiquity, and the penalties for misconduct by female deacons were far more severe than for their male counterparts. As with the other clergy in major orders, female deacons could not marry after their ordination (by contrast, members of all minor orders except subdeacons were permitted to marry) . . . Judging from the age and marital restrictions, it would appear that the purpose of these restrictions was to ensure that female deacons were as chaste and sexually nonthreatening—perhaps even asexual— as possible. This would also explain why the punishment for sexual misconduct was far harsher for deaconesses than for the male clergy, exemplified most starkly by a provision in Justinian's Novel 6, promulgated in 535, which prescribed the death penalty for any deaconess who broke her vow of celibacy by marrying or engaging in fornication." Karras, "Female Deacons," 294.

29. See *CIC*, vol. 3, *Novellae*, cited in Karras, "Female Deacons," 293.

30. Karras, "Female Deacons," 293, footnote 96.

31. Barberini, cited in Karras, "Female Deacons," 292. Karras also notes (ibid., 308) that "Perhaps the most striking aspect of the ordination rite for the female deacon, and the one that most obviously demonstrates that the female diaconate was considered a major order, is that the deaconess received the Eucharist at the altar with the rest of the higher clergy."

Confirming Argument C: Historical Theology

document, like the *Apostolic Constitutions*, also contains an ordination prayer for female deacons:

> Holy and almighty God, who through the birth of your only begotten Son and our God from the Virgin according to the flesh sanctified the female, and not to men alone but also to women bestowed grace and the advent of your Holy Spirit; now, Lord, look upon this your servant and call her to the work of your diaconate, and send down upon her the abundant gift of your Holy Spirit; keep her in orthodox faith, in blameless conduct, always fulfilling her ministry according to your pleasure; because to you is due all glory and honor.[32]

The early church practice of sending deaconesses to distribute the elements of the Lord's Table (*Didascalia Apostolorum* 16) apparently continued into the ninth century.[33] Photios (c. 810–93), the Patriarch of Constantinople, wrote a letter to bishop Leo of Italy regarding Christian women who took Communion to believers in prison, telling Leo to choose noble women "worthy of being received into the diaconate and of being received into the rank of deacons."[34] Although Leo apparently knew little about women deacons, Photios was familiar with the tasks and qualifications for deaconesses.

Also from the ninth century was Irene of Chrysabalanton, an ordained nun and deaconess of Hagia Sophia.[35]

---

32. Bar. 163.3, in *Barberini*, 185–86; Goar, *Euchologion*, 218; Bradshaw, *Ordination Rites*, 138, all cited in Karras, "Female Deacons," 300.

33. In reflecting on this matter, Blomberg (a complementarian) says in Beck, *Two Views*, 154, "Complementarians and egalitarians alike should thus be able to agree that women and men both will serve Communion (the Lord's Supper, Eucharist)."

34. Photios, *Photii patriarchae Constantinopolitani*, 166, cited in Karras, "Female Deacons," 278.

35. After citing Irene's tenth century hagiographer, Karras says "Three things are notable in the above account: (1) the (masculine) second declension noun *diakonos* (διάκονος) was still being used, rather than the feminized *diakonissa* (διακόνισσα); (2) the word *cheirotonia* (χειροτονία) was used, a technical term for ordination; and (3) Irene was simultaneously consecrated as *hegoumene*, or abbess, of her monastery. The use of the title *diakonos* is significant since the alternative title, *diakonissa*, could also refer to the wife

63

A Case for Female Deacons

Karras notes particular activities of female deacons in the 900s:

> A liturgical manual from the Church of Jerusalem dating to the tenth century includes in its paschal rubrics two orders of ordained or consecrated women: female deacons and *myrophoroi* (myrrhbearers). According to the rubrics, near the end of the paschal matins there was a procession to the solea, which included two of various orders of clergy: deacons, subdeacons, *myrophoroi*, and deaconesses. While the *myrophoroi* followed behind the deacons, holding three-legged reading stands *(triskellia)*, the deaconesses carried two *manoualia* (single candleholders) with lit candles. In general, however, female deacons did not have the public processional and other liturgical functions of male deacons.[36]

In 1018, "Pope Benedict VIII conferred on the cardinal bishop of Porto the right to ordain bishops, priests, deacons, deaconesses, subdeacons, churches, and altars."[37] The ordination of abbesses during this period was also apparently not uncommon.[38]

About a century later there appear visible signs of the decline in the ordination of deaconesses. Probably referring to certain groups of monastic women, the Greek Orthodox canonist Theodore Balsamon commented, "[t]oday deaconesses are no longer ordained although certain members of ascetical religious communities are erroneously styled deaconesses."[39] Non-ordained female deacons were still active in the Eastern Church at this time.

---

of a deacon. Both the saint's personal background—Irene was a nun with no former husband—and the term *diakonos* make it patent that the patriarch was indeed ordaining Irene to a clerical order. Her ordained status is further reinforced both by the use of the term *cheirotonia* for "ordination" (the significance of which will be discussed in Section V) and by the patriarch's beginning the Divine Liturgy, the liturgical context for ordinations to major orders." Karras, "Female Deacons," 280.

36. Karras, "Female Deacones," 285.
37. Macy, "Ordination of Women," 481–507.
38. Ibid.
39. Balsamon, *Scholia in Concilium Chalcedonense*, in Karras, "Female Deacons," 284.

CONFIRMING ARGUMENT C: HISTORICAL THEOLOGY

WYCLIF TO TURRETIN

With the role of deaconesses and abbesses generally fading from the scene during the later periods of the medieval church, and with the rise of the great schisms from Luther's time to the death of Calvin, female deacons become more difficult to find in the story of Christian ecclesiology. During the Reformation era, female deacons are more of the exception than the norm. Nevertheless, female deacons do appear in churches and are affirmed in theological literature during this period.

While the French Reformer John Calvin (1509-64) believed that the "women" in 1 Tim 3:11 refers to deacons wives,[40] he seems to affirm that Phoebe was indeed an "official" deacon in Rom 16:1-2:

> He first commends to them Phoebe, to whom he gave this Epistle to be brought to them; and, in the first place, he commends her on account of her office, for she performed a most honorable and a most holy function in the Church; and then he adduces another reason why they ought to receive her and to show her every kindness, for she had always been a helper to all the godly.[41]

Calvin also clarifies the function of deaconesses in one of the most important theological works of the Reformation, *The Institutes of the Christian Religion*:

> Deaconesses were created not to appease God with songs or unintelligible mumbling, not to live the rest of the time in idleness, but to discharge the public ministry of the church toward the poor and to strive with all zeal, constancy, and diligence in the task of love.[42]

Despite Calvin's clear affirmation of female deacons and their "public" role, it is unfortunate that few Reformed churches followed up on this aspect of his theology. In fact, few Reformed

---

40. Calvin, *First Epistle to Timothy*, 87.
41. Calvin, "Commentary on Romans."
42. Calvin, *Institutes of the Christian Religion*, iv.xiii.19.

churches even applied his teaching about deacons in general. P. Benedict explains:

> The distinction Calvin made between two kinds of deacons, those who collected alms and those who distributed them, rarely survived in the larger Reformed churches. Only a very few churches likewise actualized the possibility that he mentioned in his theological writings that women might fill this ministry. For Lambert Daneau in the late sixteenth century, the disappearance of deaconesses since the time of the primitive church was a fortunate development that demonstrated how features of the early church might wisely be discarded. The seventeenth century Parisian pastor [and friend of Francis Turretin] Jean Daillé was more willing to imply that this might have been a laudable institution.[43] Neither, however, betrayed any awareness of Reformed churches in their lifetimes that actually had deaconesses. In fact, the churches of Amsterdam, Wesel, and perhaps several other cities of the Rhineland did institute such a post to attend to the needs of poor widows and single women, but they were exceptional in doing so.[44]

Some scholars note that Calvin's companion, Martin Bucer (1491-1551), legitimized the ministry of deaconesses in Strasbourg:

> In Strasbourg, Martin Bucer successfully urged the city to create lay committees in each parish, called *Kirchenpfleger*, to be responsible for moral and religious improvement. In 1532 these *Kirchenpfleger* recommended that deacons and deaconesses be chosen to care for the poor and sick, a ministry similar to the ministry in the early church.[45]

---

43. It is uncertain what Benedict is exactly referring to, but it could be the following words of Daillé: "In certain places it will also be suitable, we think, that women of approved faith and probity and advanced age be admitted to this office, according to the example of the apostles," *Acta Synodi Wesaliensis*, Richter 2:315, cited in McKee, *Diaconate and Liturgical Almsgiving*, 221.

44. Benedict, *Christ's Churches Purely Reformed*, 455.

45. Yrigoyen, "Office of Deacon," 327-42. Cf. Olson, *Deacons and*

Confirming Argument C: Historical Theology

The Huguenot landowner Jean Morély wrote a substantial work to challenge the Presbyterian-synodal system first inaugurated around 1559. His *Treatise of Christian Discipline and Governance* (1562) included an argument for the inclusion of women in church orders. He apparently "wished to reinstitute the order of deaconesses found in the early church. These women would serve, in contrast to the 'lazy' order of nuns, as a group dedicated to social service, such as the care of the sick and the poor."[46] Unfortunately, this recommendation was overshadowed by the rest of the book's assertions, which were considered by many at the time as radical, leading to Morély's excommunication (though he was later readmitted).[47]

Theodore Beza (1519–1605), Calvin's successor at Geneva, followed the lead of others in saying that the widows in 1 Tim 5:9–10 are speaking of "deaconesses":

> For in this place the apostle is concerned with those widows whose activities were employed particularly for the care of the sick and poor, and who are called deaconesses in ecclesiastical history. This καταλεγέσθω signifies to be recruited into the office and into the group.[48]

In England under Queen Elizabeth, a group of "non-conformist ministers" gathered together to draw up ecclesiastical guidelines in 1576. One of these guidelines specified:

Deaconesses, 121.

46. Haldane and Coon, *That Gentle Strength*, 163.

47. "In some regards, Morély's proposals for the congregational election of pastors and for open discussion of doctrinal issues in a congregational *prophétie* resemble the practices of the strangers' churches of London, which he knew. But he went well beyond a Lasco in his faith in the indwelling of the Spirit within the visible church. Indeed, Morély's proposals seemed dangerously impractical, anarchic, and democratic to Calvin and Beza, who now rallied strongly to the defense of the system established in France—on prudential rather than *jure divino* grounds. *Treatise on the Discipline and Christian Government* was burned in Geneva as harmful to the church. Morély was excommunicated. The French national synod of 1562 condemned the book for its 'wicked doctrine tending to the dissipation and confusion of the church.'" Benedict, *Christ's Churches Purely Reformed*, 136.

48. Beza cited in Elsie, *Diaconate and Liturgical Almsgiving*, 219.

A Case for Female Deacons

> Touching deacons of both sorts, namely, both men and women, the Church should be admonished what is required by the apostle, that they are not to choose men by custom or course, or for their riches, but for their zeal, and integrity; and that the Church is to pray in the meantime to be so directed that they may choose them that are meet. Let the names of those that are thus chosen be published the next Lord's Day, and after that their duties to the Church, and the Church's duty toward them. Then let them be received into their office with the general prayers of the whole Church.[49]

Clearly, "deacons" were readily identifiable as "men and women."

Deaconesses apparently received mention in several Puritan contexts as well. One of them, according to a religious encyclopedia, was the Puritan church in Amsterdam:

> With the Reformation came an effort to again establish the order in the Church. In the Bohemian and Anabaptist churches deaconesses arose informally; and in the Netherlands special legislation in their favor was almost effected. In 1851, the tide turned and they were formally disapproved. In a Puritan church in Amsterdam, however, we find an ancient widow acting as deaconess as late as 1606. In England also the Puritans heartily approved of deaconesses, but in spite of ecclesiastical approval the order did not flourish.[50]

According to A. Earle, there was also an effort to institute female deacons in the New England Puritan Church:

> It was much desired by several of the first-settled ministers that there should be deaconesses in the New England Puritan church, and many good reasons were given for making such appointments. It was believed that for the special

---

49. Neal cited in Bancroft, *Deaconesses in Europe*, 142.

50. Stanford, *Encyclopedia of Religious Knowledge*, 245. Cf. Meyer, *Deaconesses, Biblical, Early Church, European, American*, 28–30 and Bancroft, *Deaconesses in Europe*, 143–144.

duty of visiting the sick and afflicted in the community deaconesses would be more useful than deacons.[51]

The recognition of female deacons in the Anabaptist tradition was more common. The deaconess appears in the Dordrecht Confession (1632) as an ordained office, being blended, as it had for centuries, with the "office" of "widow." However, while the text requires the women to be "aged," there are no specific age limitations like there are with the canons of the Council of Chalcedon. Here is the text from the Dordrecht Confession:

> IX. Of the Election, and Offices of Teachers, Deacons, and Deaconesses, in the Church
>
> And that also honorable aged widows should be chosen and ordained deaconesses, that they with the deacons may visit, comfort, and care for, the poor, feeble, sick, sorrowing and needy, as also the widows and orphans, and assist in attending to other wants and necessities of the church to the best of their ability. 1 Tim 5:9; Rom 16:1; James 1:27.[52]

TURRETIN TO BARTH: REFORMED

The final period of history that we will sketch covers the period from around 1700 to essentially the First World War. Demonstrating the activity of women deacons in this period is not difficult—especially for the Methodist and congregational churches. However, due to the substantial upsurge in deaconesses, missionaries, public preachers and pastors,[53] we will limit ourselves to the

---

51. Earle, *Sabbath in Puritan New England*, 62.

52. Leith, *Creeds of the Churches*, 301.

53. See for example, the historical accounts in chapters 9 and 10 in Husbands and Larsen, *Women, Ministry, and the Gospel*; chapter 6 in Olson, *Deacons and Deaconesses*; chapter 5 in Tucker, *Women in the Maze*. For a short account of Baptist women preachers, see McBeth, "Changing Role," 84–96, esp. 89–80, and a longer account in his work *Baptist Heritage*. For primary sources during this period in history, see MacHaffie, *Readings in Her Story*, chapters 5–9.

two particular strands of Christianity where women deacons are thought to appear less frequently: Reformed and Baptist.

Beginning with the Reformed tradition, Matthew Henry (1662–1714) refers to Phoebe as "a servant to the church at Cenchrea: *diakonon*, a servant by office, a stated servant." Henry seems to be following Calvin's lead in specifically talking about Phoebe's "office."

Jonathan Edwards (1703–58) favorably cites "D. Turner's Social Religion" when discussing deacons and the citation presumably represents his own position. Turner says:

> It is generally allowed by inquirers into these subjects, that in the primitive church there were *deaconesses*, i.e. pious women, whose particular benefits [include] entertainment and care of the itinerant preachers; visit the sick and imprisoned, instruct female catechumens, and [administer] their baptism; then more particularly necessary from the peculiar customs of those countries, the persecuted state of the church, and the speedier spreading of the gospel . . . it is reasonable to think *Phoebe* was [mentioned in Rom.xvi.1][54] who is expressly called a *deacon*, or stated servant, as Dr. Doddridge renders it. They were usually *widows*, and to prevent scandal, generally in years . . . The apostolic constitutions (as they are called) mention the ordination of a deaconess.[55]

The southern theologian Robert Dabney (1820–98) appears to take no issue with the legitimacy of deaconesses *per se* when given a clear opportunity. He mentions them in the baptism portion of his systematic theology when objecting to "sponsors":

> The use of sponsors, who are now always other than the proper parents (when any sponsors are used), in the Episcopal and Romanist Churches, has grown from gradual additions. In the early Church the sponsors were always the natural parents of the infant, except in cases of orphanage and slavery: and then they were either the master, or some deacon or deaconess. (See Bingham, p.

---

54. This bracket is in the original, while the others are not.
55. D. Turner in Edwards, *History of Redemption*, 382.

523, cf.) When an adult was *in extremis* and even speechless, or maniacal, or insensible, if it could be proved that he had desired baptism, he was permitted to receive it, and someone stood sponsor for him. If he recovered, this sponsor was expected to watch over his religious life and instruction. And in the case of Catechumens, the sponsor was at first some clergy man or deaconess, who undertook his religious guidance. It was a universal rule that no one was allowed to be sponsor unless he undertook this *bona fide*. How perverted is this usage now! Our great objection to the appearance of any one but the natural parents, where there are any, or in other cases, of him who is in *loco parentis*, as sponsors, is this: that no other human has the right to dedicate the child, and no other has the opportunity and authority to train it for God. To take these vows in any other sense is mockery.[56]

Dabney also made a remark in a sermon that sharply distinguished the role between women deacons and women preachers:

In 1 Timothy 5:9-15, a sphere of church ministry is clearly defined for older single women, and for them only, who are widows or have never been married and are without any near relatives. So specific is the apostle that he categorically fixes the limit to those sixty years old, below which the church may not accept. What was this sphere of labor? It was evidently some form of deaconess type work, helping others, and clearly not preaching, because the age, qualifications and connections all point to these private benevolent tasks, and the uninspired history confirms it.[57]

Charles Hodge (1797-1878) appears to acknowledge the legitimacy of female deacons when recognizing that some churches in the apostolic period had deaconesses, while some did not:

Even the Apostolical Churches were not all organized precisely in the same way. The presence of an Apostle, or of a man clothed with apostolical authority, as in the

---

56. Dabney, *Systematic Theology*, Lecture 63.
57. Dabney, "Women Preachers."

case of James in Jerusalem, necessarily gave to a Church a form which other churches where no Apostle permanently resided could not have. Some had deaconesses, others had not. So all churches in every age and wherever they have existed, have felt at liberty to modify their organization and modes of action so as to suit them to their peculiar circumstances. All such modifications are matters of indifference. They cannot be made to bind the conscience, nor can they be rendered conditions of Christian or ecclesiastical fellowship. As Christ is the only head of the Church it follows that its allegiance is to Him, and that whenever those out of the Church undertake to regulate its affairs or to curtail its liberties, its members are bound to obey Him rather than men.[58]

Hodge apparently believed that churches should be free to have deaconesses if they wish. In his commentary on Romans, Hodge refers to Phoebe as a "deaconess":

In This Concluding Chapter, Paul First Commends To The Church At Rome The Deaconess Phebe [sic], Vers. 1, 2. . . .It appears that in the apostolic church, elderly females were selected to attend upon the poor and sick of their own sex. Many ecclesiastical writers suppose there were two classes of these female officers; the one (πρεσβύτιδες, corresponding in some measure in their duties to the elders,) having the oversight of the conduct of the younger female Christians; and the other, whose duty was to attend to the sick and the poor.[59]

The historian Philip Schaff (1819-93) finds support for deaconesses both in 1 Tim 5 and Rom 16:

Then in verse nine and ten [of 1 Timothy 5] he then distinguishes in the circle of these pious widows a still smaller class of those who were matriculated or enrolled, and demands in them certain qualifications, which it is most natural to refer to the office of deaconess.[60] [Paul]

---

58. Hodge, *Systematic Theology*, 2.11.3.
59. Hodge, *Epistle to the Romans*.
60. Schaff, *History of the Apostolic Church*, 536.

Confirming Argument C: Historical Theology

had a favorable opportunity in the departure of the deaconess, Phoebe, from Cenchreae near Corinth for Rome (Rom. 16:1).[61]

Later, Schaff mentions Phoebe again, saying, "Rom 16:1, where even a deaconess, Phoebe, is mentioned."[62] In the first volume of his *History of the Christian Church*, Schaff again refers to "the deaconess of Phoebe" and later lists spiritual gifts, the seventh of which is "The Gift of Ministry and Help, that is, of special qualification primarily for the office of deacon and deaconess."[63]

The Dutch dogmatician Herman Bavinck (1854–1921) also has a particularly favorable stance towards female deacons:

> In considering the word *diakonia* in Acts 11:29; Romans 12:7; 1 Corinthians 12:5; 2 Corinthians 8:4; 9:1, 12, 13; Revelation 2:19; and especially in all the places where the office of deacons and deaconesses are mentioned, we must above all think of the ministry of mercy.... In 1 Timothy 3 Paul sums up their qualifications, and in Romans 16:1-2; 1 Timothy 3:11; 5:9-10, there is mention of deaconesses.[64]

Clearly, Bavinck believes that female deacons are legitimate because they are found in Scripture. His interpretation of 1 Tim 3:11 and Rom 16:1-2 are essentially the same as that in chapters 4–5 of this work.[65]

Bavinck's American friend, the apologist B. B. Warfield, argued that early church history confirms that Rom 16:1 speaks of Phoebe as a deaconess:

> For it need not be denied that the office of deaconess is a Scriptural office, although it must be confessed

---

61. Ibid., 298.
62. Ibid., 355, footnote 1.
63. Schaff, *History of the Christian Church*, 1:104, 117.
64. Bavinck, *Reformed Dogmatics*, 4:346–47.
65. Van Driel, "Status of Women in Contemporary Society," 153–95: "[Bavinck] wrote sympathetically about efforts to restore the office of deaconess in the churches of the Reformation. In fact only the offices of minister and elder to Bavinck seemed clearly exempt for women."

that the Biblical warrant for it is . . . the slenderest . . . Phoebe might have been only an humble "servant" of the Cenchrean church, or indeed, for all that the term itself declares, only a Christian belonging to that church (cf. John 12:26). Nor is there any compelling reason apparent in the context, shutting us up to the technical sense of "deaconess." Nevertheless this seems the more likely meaning of the phrase; and this interpretation receives confirmation from a clear indication, coming to us from the earliest post-apostolic times, that "deaconesses" were then already an established order in the church. . . . We need not doubt, then, that the church has a distinct right to organize the work of woman after either of the fashions toward which the minds of Presbyterians turn when they speak of "deaconesses."[66]

Princeton Seminary professor A. T. McGill tried to revive the office of deaconess. Though he didn't believe 1 Tim 3:11 refers to women deacons, he still argued that women should have church office, as allowed for in his church's constitution:[67]

> If the people of particular church would simply elect women as well as men to the office of deacon, making on board or two separate boards, at their pleasure, as now provided in our constitution, the order is restored.[68]

Warfield suggested a wider application of McGill's recommendations:

> Probably more than one Presbyterian congregation in America has already acted more or less in the sense of Dr. McGill's suggestion. Dr. George O. Hays, on the floor of the Belfast Council, in 1884, announced himself as the happy pastor who possessed twenty-four deaconesses. In 1881 the Corinthian Avenue Presbyterian Church of Philadelphia, under an impulse received from a visit from the younger Fliedner, placed the care of their poor

---

66. Warfield, "Presbyterian Deaconesses," 283–93.
67. McGill, cited in Warfield, "Presbyterian Deaconesses," 287. Cf. Olson, *Deacons and Deaconesses*, 293.
68. Warfield, "Presbyterian Deaconesses," 287.

and sick in the hands of "five deaconesses," reviving (so it is phrased) the work, but not the office. More recently, the Third Presbyterian Church of Los Angeles, California, empowered its three deacons to choose three women from congregation to co-operate with them in their work, granting them seats and votes in the board's monthly meeting. These are probably only examples of what has been done in many congregations, although thus far without sanction from the higher courts of the church. Perhaps the nearest approach to the more formal and ecclesiastical revival of the office among us, in its proper Scriptural sense, has been made by the Southern Presbyterian Church, which sets forth in its *Book of Church Order*, adopted in 1879, that "where it shall appear needful, the Church Session may select and appoint godly women for the care of the sick, of prisoners, of poor widows and orphans, and in general for the relief of distress." Here we have the essential features of the office.[69]

TURRETIN TO BARTH: BAPTIST

Moving to the Baptist tradition, the Baptist particularist John Smyth (often referred to as the "founder" of the Baptists) affirmed deaconesses as well as their ordination. His writing in 1607 affirmed the early church tradition of grouping deaconesses and widows into the same class, and limited their age to sixty years of age (cf. Theodosius prior to the Council of Nicaea).[70] Their work was to relieve "the bodily infirmities of the Saints."[71] Later on, he affirmed the ordination of deaconesses.[72]

Thomas Helwys, an English Baptist separatist, wrote a confession in 1611 that functioned as the groundwork for the First

69. Ibid.

70. See Leonard, *Baptist Ways*, 56.

71. Smyth, *Works of John Smyth*, 1:259–60, cited in Deweese, "Deaconesses in Baptist History," 51–57.

72. Ibid., 2:509.

Baptist Confession. In his confession he expressed support for female deacons:

> That the officers of every Church or congregation are either elders, who by their office do especially feed the flock concerning their souls, or deacons, men, and women who by their office relieve the necessities of the poor and impotent brethren concerning their bodies.[73]

Charles Deweese finds active deaconesses in the 1660s at a church in Bristol.[74] Generally speaking, there were apparently very few women deacons in America during the 1600s, but deaconesses can be found in the 1700s in Virginia, North Carolina, and South Carolina. Most of these records depend on the work of Morgan Edwards, who himself "favored them and identified Romans 16:1 and 1 Timothy 3:11 as biblical bases for them," and saw them as directed "chiefly . . . to those things wherefore men are less fit."[75]

The great Sandy Creek Church in North Carolina, which spawned forty-two other churches and over a hundred ministers, had deaconesses.[76] In the 1800s, several prominent Baptist pastors affirmed that Scripture provides support for deaconesses, such as E. Hiscox (1894), E. Dargan (1897), and the Southern Baptist Convention framer R. Howell (1846).[77] In the 1900s, F. Agar (1923),[78] A. T. Robertson (1931),[79] and J. R. Graves[80] were favorable towards

---

73. Helwys, "Thomas Helwys' Confession."

74. Deweese, "Deaconesses in Baptist History," 53. Cf. McBeth, "The Changing Role of Women in Baptist History," 84–96.

75. Deweese, "Deaconesses in Baptist History," 54.

76. Ibid., 55–56.

77. "Take all these passages together [Rom 16:1–2, 1 Tim 3:11 and 5:9–10], and I think it will be difficult for us to resist the conclusion that the word of God authorizes, and in some sense, certainly by implication, enjoins the appointment of deaconesses in the churches of Christ . . . Deaconesses, therefore, are everywhere, as necessary as they were in the days of the apostles." Howell, cited in McBeth, *Baptist Heritage*, 690.

78. Deweese, "Deaconesses in Baptist History," 56–57.

79. See Robertson, *Word Pictures in the New Testament*, 4:425.

80. McBeth, *Women in Baptist Life*, 142: "There is no doubt in the minds of Biblical and ecclesiastical scholars, that in the apostolic churches women

CONFIRMING ARGUMENT C: HISTORICAL THEOLOGY

deaconesses. According to J. Denison, largely leaning on McBeth's work *The Baptist Heritage*, "B. H. Carroll recognized women deacons in First Baptist Church of Waco, Texas. He thought that 1 Timothy 3:11 should be translated 'women deacons' and not 'wives.'"[81]

McBeth's own conclusion brings our study to a close:

> The evidence suggests that in the nineteenth century many Southern Baptists approved deaconesses and regarded the offices as biblical. Moreover, at least some churches acted upon these views and regularly set aside deaconesses as well as deacons. Probably Southern Baptist churches have never been without deaconesses.[82]

CONCLUSION

Our brief survey of church history leads us to conclude that female deacons have been active, recognized servants of God throughout virtually every major period of the church. Furthermore, Christian leaders were willing to stand up for the legitimacy of female deacons even when the rest of the church didn't—precisely because they found female deacons to be a Scriptural and edifying to the church. In particular, supporters appealed to one or more of the following passages: Rom 16:1–2, 1 Tim 3:11; and 1 Tim 5:9.

Those who believed in the scriptural legitimacy of female deacons were not isolated to one tradition or one period of history. Deaconesses were recognized in practice, in theological formulations, and even in the texts of the great ecumenical councils of Nicaea and Chalcedon. They continued to be recognized and appreciated in the Eastern churches of the Byzantine era up to the Reformation. During the Reformation, support of women deacons

---

occupied the office of the deaconship . . . Phoebe was a deaconess of the church in Cenchrea."

81. Denison, "Should Women Serve as Deacons?"

82. McBeth, *Women in Baptist Life*, 143, cited in Denison, "Should Women be Deacons?" 21. Blomberg grieves the situation in Beck, *Two Views*, 148: ". . . sadly, very few Southern Baptists allow for women deacons."

appeared in Anabaptist confessions (Dordrecht) and in great theological works (such as Calvin's *Institutes*). From then on, support for deaconesses appeared in virtually every church tradition, including Baptist, Presbyterian, Methodist, and Congregational. Contrary to the suspicions of many today, female deacons were at home in both the Reformed and Baptist traditions.

6

Conclusion

Therefore, the truthfulness of conclusion (2) is reaffirmed by the testimony of the Scriptures (namely, Rom 16:1–2, 1 Tim 3:11) and of the church.

THE FOLLOWING ARGUMENT HAS been made:

1. (Primary Premise) The ban on women elders propounded by complementarians does not apply to women deacons; the Scriptures teach that teaching and exercising authority over men is neither a required ability nor necessary task undertaken by a deacon (whether "functional" or "official").
2. (Primary Conclusion) Therefore, the office of deacon is not gender specific and qualified women are encouraged to occupy it.
   a. (Confirming Argument A) The New Testament authors show awareness of women deacons in Rom 16:1.
   b. (Confirming Argument B) The Apostle Paul provides the qualifications of women deacons in 1 Tim 3:11.
   c. (Confirming Argument C) Female deacons ("deaconesses") are not foreign to church history. Rather, female deacons have been conceptually approved by Christian leaders and have actually existed in many churches throughout history.

3. (Final Conclusion) Therefore, the truthfulness of conclusion (2) is reaffirmed by the testimony of the scriptures (namely, Rom. 16:1–2, 1 Tim. 3:11) and by the church.

The implications of this argument are clear: if the Bible, as supported by the various testimonies of God's people through history, provides for women to be deacons, there is no good reason to ban women from occupying the office of deacon on the basis of their sex. Contemporary churches that confess the Reformation doctrine of *sola scriptura* should seriously consider revisiting their church constitutions and traditions (and most importantly, their attitudes) to avoid the unbiblical practice of prohibiting female deacons.

CASE STUDIES AND CONCLUSION

The bylaws of one particular Reformed Baptist church provide a good example of poor ecclesiology:

> Eligibility for Office or Special Positions of Appointment:
> One must be a male member in this church in order to be considered for the office of either elder or deacon. Special assistant positions such as church secretary may be filled by either male or female.[1]

The twenty-seven-page document is replete with thorough instruction. There are biblical references provided for almost every paragraph in the work, citing Scripture for even the most narrow and subjective topics like "The Privilege and Duty of Using the Response Sheets," "The Annual Business Meeting," "Changing These Bylaws," "Churchmanship Following Baptism," and "Temporary Reception by Transfer." Yet, there is not even *one* biblical reference in the document for limiting half the congregation from the office of deacon to males only. It is clear that *sola scriptura* is not being practiced across the board.

---

1. "Bylaws of Providence Reformed Baptist Church." (Caputa, SD, 2005). Article 5, section E, subsection 1, paragraph F.

Conclusion

Other churches are not so presumptuous and attempt to provide biblical support for their position. Here is one particular example:

> While we acknowledge the valuable gifts which God has given women and the valuable assistance they may render to the officers of the church (Rom. 16:1–6; Phil. 4:3; 1 Tim. 3:11), the Bible prohibits women from holding either the office of deacon or elder in the church (1 Cor 14:33b–35; 1 Tim 2:8–15; 3:1–7).[2]

The references provided in the first half of this sentence do not support the statement that precedes them. Neither Phoebe (Rom 16:1–2) nor Euodia and Syntyche (Phil 4:3) are presented as mere assistants to church officers. Rather, they are primarily assistants (and "servant-leaders") of the *church*. Furthermore, it is misleading to limit the ministry of these women to helping "officers of the church" and cite passages about Paul since Paul wasn't even an elder or deacon of a local church himself, but a traveling missionary. Even as one in the "office" of the Apostle, it is superbly difficult to think that Paul would have supported such a simple, blanket prohibition given the substantial public praise he gave to such women as Phoebe and Junia (Rom 16:1–2, 7).

The second part of the sentence apparently assumes that 1 Tim 3:11 isn't speaking of women deacons. We refuted this assumption in chapter 5. (Ironically, then, the proof-text contradicts the point being made). The constitution also cites 1 Tim 2:8–15 and 3:1–7 in support of their prohibition, but neither text actually addresses deacons nor in any clear way substantiates the prohibition of women deacons.

It appears, then, that even when governing authorities of local churches attempt to restrict the ministries of women, they

---

2. This paragraph is found in the public constitutions of the following churches: Reformed Baptist Church of Riverside, (Riverside, CA); Grace Reformed Baptist Church (Mebane, NC); Albuquerque Sovereign Grace Baptist Church (Albuquerque, NM); Grace Reformed Church (Clarkston, WA); Grace Fellowship Church (West Toronto, Ontario); Cornerstone Bible Church (Ridgecrest, CA); Cornerstone Baptist Church (Wylie, TX).

forfeit sound exegesis and logic in the process. Perhaps there is more at play than just reading the Bible and applying it—like politics, sexism, and complacency, to name a few. In any case, it is truly amazing that such poorly constructed church laws have found their way into countless church constitutions across the globe. The paragraph ought to be erased.

As mentioned before, Capitol Hill Baptist Church is a notable example of a church that (generally)[3] offers a better alternative:

> The office of deacon is described in I Timothy 3:8–13 and Acts 6:1–7. The church shall recognize, in accordance with the constitutional provisions on elections, men and women who are giving of themselves in service to the church, and who possess particular gifts of service. These members shall be received as gifts of Christ to His church and set apart as deacons and deaconesses. They shall be elected to one term lasting for a maximum of three years and may only be elected to another term after one year.[4]

City Church of San Francisco, California (RCA), describes deacons on their website in the following way:

> The women and men elected to be deacons at City Church serve the church behind the scenes, confidentially helping our people in crisis periods of their lives. Deacons serve the social, emotional, physical, financial, and spiritual needs of the congregation. They provide financial assistance for rent, food, counseling and medical assistance, utilities, and other expenses. Much of their time is spent in prayer with and for their clients, building relationships with them, encouraging and counseling them with budget and basic life skills. People request the deacons for spiritual and practical help. Often the practical help offered is financial, made possible by your contributions to the Deacon Fund. This fund is separate from the operating budget of City Church and goes

---

3. It is disputable whether Acts 6 describes the "office" of deacon.
4. "Constitution," article 5, section 8.

CONCLUSION

directly to assist members of the congregation who find themselves in need.[5]

One could list numerous other examples. At any rate, it is encouraging to see church documents and websites like these since they embody a more biblical perspective on deacons. One can only pray that more churches will seek to challenge their own traditions and reform their theology and ecclesiology in the same manner.

---

5. "Our Deacons."

Bibliography

Agan, Clarence, III. "Deacons, Deaconesses, and Denominational Discussions: Rom 16:1 as a Test Case." *Presbyterion* 34:2 (2008) 93–108.
Allison, Gregg. *Historical Theology*. Grand Rapids: Zondervan, 2011.
Allison, Gregg, and John Feinberg. *Sojourners and Strangers: A Doctrine of the Church*. Wheaton: Crossway, 2012.
Anyabwile, Thabiti. "I'm a Complementarian, But . . . Women Can Be Deacons." *The Pure Church*, February 4, 2011. http://thegospelcoalition.org/blogs/thabitianyabwile/ 2011/02/04/im-a-complementarian-but-women-can-be-deacons.
Bancroft, Jane Marie. *Deaconesses in Europe and Their Lessons for America*. New York: Hunt & Eaton, 1889.
Barnett, James Monroe. *The Diaconate*. New York: Seaburg, 1981.
Barnett, Paul. "Wives and Women's Ministry." *The Evangelical Quarterly* 61 (1989) 232.
Bauckham, Richard. *Gospel Women: Studies in the Named Women in the Gospels*. Grand Rapids: Eerdmans, 2002.
Bavinck, Herman. *Reformed Dogmatics: Holy Spirit, Church, and New Creation*. Vol. 4. Translated by John Vriend. Grand Rapids: Baker, 2008.
Beck, James, et al., eds. *Two Views of Women in Ministry*. Grand Rapids: Zondervan, 2005.
Belleville, Linda. "Iounian . . . episemoi en tois apostolois: A Re-examination of Romans 16.7 in Light of Primary Source Materials." *New Testament Studies* 51:2 (2005) 231–49.
Benedict, Philip. *Christ's Churches Purely Reformed: A Social History of Calvinism*. London: Yale University Press, 2002.
Biblical Studies Press. *NET Bible*. 1st ed. Spokane, WA: Biblical Studies, 2006.
Blackburn, Barry. "The Identity of the 'Women' in 1 Tim 3:11." Vol. 1. In *Essays on Women in Earliest Christianity*, edited Carroll D. Osburn. Joplin, MO: College Press, 1993.
———. *I Corinthians*. NIVAC. Grand Rapids: Zondervan, 1994.
Bock, Darrel. *Acts*. BECNT. Grand Rapids: Eerdmans 2007.
———. *A Theology of Luke and Acts*. Grand Rapids: Zondervan, 2012.

BIBLIOGRAPHY

Brakel, Wilhelmus à. *A Christian's Reasonable Service*. Vol. 2. Edited by Joel Beeke. Rotterdam: D. Bolle, 1992.

Bruce, F. F. *Romans*. TNTC. Rev. ed. Grand Rapids: Eerdmans, 1985.

Buchheimer, L. B. "Highlights in the History of the Female Diaconate." *Concordia Theological Monthly* 21:4 (1950) 276–83.

Calvin, John. *Commentary on the First Epistle to Timothy*. 22 vols. Translated by William Pringle. Grand Rapids: Baker, 1981.

———. "Commentary on Romans." *Christian Classics Ethereal Library*, June 1, 2005. http://www.ccel.org/ccel/calvin/calcom38.toc.html.

———. *Institutes of the Christian Religion*. Library of Christian Classics. Translated by Ford Lewis Battles. Louisville, KY: Westminster John Knox, 1960.

Carson, Donald and Douglas J. Moo. *Introduction to the New Testament*. 2nd ed. Grand Rapids: Zondervan, 2005.

Ciampa, Roy and Brian Rosner. *The First Letter to the Corinthians*. PNTC. Edited by D. A. Carson. Grand Rapids: Eerdmans, 2010.

Clark, E. A. *Women in the Early Church*. Wilmington, DE: Michael Glazier, 1983.

Clark, Stephen B. *Man and Woman in Christ*. Lansing, MI: Tabor, 1980.

Clowney, Edmund. *The Church*. Downers Grove, IL: InterVarsity, 1995.

Cole, R. A. *Exodus: An Introduction and Commentary*. Downers Grove, IL: InterVarsity, 2008.

"Constitution of the Capitol Hill Baptist Church." *Capitol Hill Baptist,* March 15, 2009. http://www.capitolhillbaptist.org/wp-content/uploads/CHBC_Constitution.pdf.

Dabney, R. L. *Systematic Theology*. London: Banner of Truth Trust: 1985.

———. "Women Preachers: The Public Preaching of Women." *BibleBB*, October 1879. http://www.biblebb.com/files/RD-001WP.htm.

Denison, Jim. "Should Women Serve as Deacons? Seeking the Word and Will of God." *Center for Informed Faith*. http://www.godissues.org/pdf/Women_deacons.pdf.

Denney, James. *St. Paul's Epistle to the Romans*. The Expositor's Greek Testament. Grand Rapids: Eerdmans, 1979.

Deweese, Charles W. "Deaconesses in Baptist History: A Preliminary Study." *Baptist History and Heritage* 12:1 (1977) 51–57.

Dibelius, Martin, and Hans Conzelmann. *The Pastoral Epistles*. Minneapolis: Fortress, 1989.

Doriani, Paul. *Women and Ministry: What the Bible Teaches*. Wheaton, IL: Crossway, 2003.

Dunn, James. *Romans 9–16*. WBC. Vol. 38. Nashville: Thomas Nelson, 1988.

Earle, Alice M. *Sabbath in Puritan New England*. Echo Library, 2007.

Edwards, Jonathan. *The History of Redemption*. New York: T. & J. Swords, 1773.

Engle, Paul, ed. *Who Runs the Church?: Four Views on Church Government*. Grand Rapids: Zondervan, 2004.

Epp, Eldon. *Junia: The First Female Apostle*. Minneapolis: Fortress, 2005.

BIBLIOGRAPHY

Fee, Gordon. *The First Epistle to the Corinthians*. NICNT. Edited by Gordon Fee. Grand Rapids: Eerdmans, 1987.

Frame, John. *The Doctrine of the Christian Life*. Phillipsburg, NJ: P & R, 2008.

Garland, David E. *1 Corinthians*. BECNT. Grand Rapids: Eerdmans, 2003.

Gibson, Margaret. *The Didascalia Apostolorum in English*. London: Cambridge University Press, 1903.

Glasscock, Ed. "The Biblical Concept of Elder." *Bibliotheca Sacra* 144 (1987) 66–78.

Grudem, Wayne. *Systematic Theology*. Grand Rapids: Zondervan, 2000.

Grudem, Wayne, and J. I. Packer, eds. *The ESV Study Bible*. Wheaton, IL: Crossway, 2008.

Gryson, Roger. *The Ministry of Women in the Early Church*. Collegeville, MN: Liturgical, 1976.

Guthrie, Donald. *The Pastoral Epistles*. TNTC. Edited by Leon Morris. Downers Grove, IL: InterVarsity, 2009.

Haldane, Katherine, and Lynda Coon. *That Gentle Strength: Historical Perspectives on Women in Christianity*. Charlottesville, VA: University of Virginia Press, 1990.

Hamilton, James, Jr. "What Women Can Do in Ministry." In *Women, Ministry and the Gospel*, edited by Mark Husbands and Timothy Larsen. Downers Grove, IL: InterVarsity, 2007.

Helwys, Thomas. "Thomas Helwys' Confession, 1611." *Baptist Studies Online*. http://baptiststudiesonline.com/wp-content/uploads/2007/08/helwys-confession.PDF.

Hodge, Charles. *Systematic Theology*. New York: Scribner, 1960.

———. *A Commentary on Paul's Epistle to the Romans*. Grand Rapids: Eerdmans, 1994.

Hurley, James B. *Man and Woman in Biblical Perspective*. Grand Rapids: Zondervan, 1981.

Husbands, Mark, and Timothy Larsen. *Women, Ministry, and the Gospel: Exploring New Paradigms*. Downers Grove, IL: IVP Academic, 2007.

Karras, Valerie. "Female Deacons in the Byzantine Church." *Church History* 73:2 (2004) 271–31.

Keener, Craig S. *The InterVarsity Bible Background Commentary: New Testament*. Downers Grove, IL: InterVarsity, 1993.

Kelly, Douglas. *Systematic Theology*. Vol. 1. Scotland: Christian Focus, 2008.

Kent, Homer. *The Pastoral Epistles*. Chicago: Moody, 1958.

Kistemaker, Simon J. *1 Corinthians*. NTC. Grand Rapids: Baker, 1994.

Knight George. *The Pastoral Epistles: A Commentary on the Greek Text*. NIGTC. Edited by I. Howard Marshall and Donald Hagner. Grand Rapids: Eerdmans, 1999.

Köstenberger, Andreas J. "A Complex Sentence." In *Women in the Church: An Analysis and Application of 1 Timothy 2:9–15*, edited by Andreas J. Köstenberger and Thomas R. Schreiner. Grand Rapids: Baker, 2005.

BIBLIOGRAPHY

Köstenberger, Andreas J., and Terry Wilder, eds. *Entrusted with the Gospel: Paul's Theology in the Pastoral Epistles.* Nashville: Broadman & Holman, 2010.

Kroll, Guilelmus, and Rudolf Schoell, eds. *Novellae.* Berlin: Weidmann, 1959.

Kruse, Colin. *Paul's Letter to the Romans*, PNTC. Grand Rapids: Eerdmans, 2012.

Ladd, George. *A Theology of the New Testament.* Rev. ed. Grand Rapids: Eerdmans, 1993.

"Led." *Capitol Hill Baptist.* http://www.capitolhillbaptist.org/we-are/led/.

Leith, John H., ed. *Creeds of the Churches.* 3rd ed. Louisville, KY: Westminster John Knox, 1982.

Lenski, R. C. H. *The Interpretation of St. Paul's Epistles to the Colossians, to the Thessalonians, to Timothy, to Titus and to Philemon.* Minneapolis: Augsburg, 1961.

Leonard, Bill. *Baptist Ways: A History.* Valley Forge, PA: Judson, 2003.

Lewis, Robert M. "The 'Women' of 1 Tim 3:11." *Bibliotheca Sacra* 146:542 (1979) 167–75.

Liefield, Walter. "The Nature of Authority in the New Testament." In *Discovering Biblical Equality*, edited by Ronald Pierce and Rebecca Groothuis. Downers Grove, IL: InterVarsity, 2005.

Lightfoot, Joseph Barber. *Saint Paul's Epistle to the Philippians: A Revised Text with Introduction, Notes, and Dissertations.* Grand Rapids, Zondervan, 1956.

MacArthur, John. *1 Timothy*, MacArthur New Testament Commentary. Chicago: Moody, 1995.

———. *Answering the Key Questions about Elders.* Panorama City, CA: Word of Grace Communications, 1984.

———. *John MacArthur Study Bible.* NASB. Nashville: Thomas Nelson, 2006.

MacHaffie, Barbara. *Readings in Her Story.* Minneapolis: Fortress, 1992.

Macy, Gary. "The Ordination of Women in the Early Middle Ages." *Theological Studies* 61:3 (2000) 481–507.

Madsen, Thorvald, II, "The Ethics of the Pastoral Epistles." In *Entrusted with the Gospel: Paul's Theology in the Pastoral Epistles*, edited by Andreas Köstenberger and Terry Wilder. Nashville: B & H, 2010.

Mappes, David. "The Elder in the Old and New Testaments," *Bibliotheca Sacra* 154 (1997) 80–88.

Marshall, Howard. *Acts.* TNTC. Edited by Leon Morris. Grand Rapids: InterVarsity, 2008.

Mathew, Susan. "Women in the Greetings of Rom. 16:1–16: A Study of Mutuality and Women's Ministry in the Letter to the Romans." PhD diss., Durham University, 2010.

McBeth, Leon. *The Baptist Heritage.* Nashville: Broadman, 1987.

———. "The Changing Role of Women in Baptist History." *Southwestern Journal of Theology* 22:1 (1979) 84–96.

———. *Women in Baptist Life.* Nashville: Broadman, 1979.

BIBLIOGRAPHY

McKee, Elsie. *John Calvin on the Diaconate and Liturgical Almsgiving.* Geneva: Librairie Droz, 1984.

Meyer, Lucy. *Deaconesses, Biblical, Early Church, European, American.* Cincinnati: Cranston and Stowe, 1892.

Moo, Douglas J. *The Epistle to the Romans.* NICNT. Edited by Gordon Fee. Grand Rapids: Eerdmans, 1996.

———. *The Letters to the Colossians and to Philemon.* PNTC. Edited by D. A. Carson. Eerdmans: Grand Rapids, 2008.

Morris, Leon. *The Epistle to the Romans.* PNTC. Edited by D. A. Carson. Grand Rapids: Eerdmans, 1988.

Mounce, William C. *Pastoral Epistles.* WBC. Edited by David Hubbard, Bruce Metzger, and Glenn Barker. Nashville: Thomas Nelson, 2000.

———. "1 Tim. 3:2—Can an Elder be Divorced?" *Koinonia*, March 9, 2009. http://www.koinoniablog.net/2009/03/can-an-elder-be-divorced.html.

Newsom, Carol, and Sharon Ringe. *The Women's Bible Commentary.* Louisville, NY: Westminster John Knox, 1992.

Olson, Jeannine. *Deacons and Deaconesses Throughout the Centuries.* Rev. ed. St. Louis: Concordia, 2005.

"Our Deacons." *City Church San Francisco.* http://www.citychurchsf.org/Deacons.

Payne, Philip. *Man and Woman, One in Christ.* Grand Rapids: Zondervan, 2009.

Perry, Gregory. "Phoebe and Cenchreae and 'Women' of Ephesus." *Presbyterion* 36:1 (2010) 9–36.

Peterson, David. *The Acts of the Apostle.* PNTC. Edited by D. A. Carson. Grand Rapids: Eerdmans, 2009.

Piper, John. "What Did Deacons Do?" *Desiring God Ministries*, March 9, 1987. http://www.desiringgod.org/sermons/what-did-deacons-do.

Piper, John, and Wayne A. Grudem. *Recovering Biblical Manhood and Womanhood: A Response to Evangelical Feminism.* Wheaton, IL: Crossway, 1991.

Ranft, Patricia. *Women and the Religious Life in Premodern Europe.* New York: Saint Martin's Press, 1998.

Reymond, Robert. *A New Systematic Theology of the Christian Faith.* Rev. ed. Nashville: Thomas Nelson, 1998.

Robertson, A. T. *Word Pictures in the New Testament.* Nashville: Broadman, 1930.

Stanford, Elias. *A Concise Encyclopedia of Religious Knowledge.* Hartford: Scranton, 1912.

Saucy, Robert, and Judish Tenelshof, eds. *Women and Men in Ministry: A Complementary Perspective.* Chicago: Moody, 2001.

Schaff, Philip. *The History of the Apostolic Church.* New York: Scribner, 1853.

———. *The History of the Christian Church.* Vol. 2. New York: Scribner, 1884.

Schreiner, Thomas R. *Romans.* BECNT. Grand Rapids: Baker Academic, 1998.

BIBLIOGRAPHY

———. "The Valuable Ministries of Women in the Context of Male Leadership." In *Recovering Biblical Manhood and Womanhood*, edited by John Piper and Wayne Grudem. Wheaton, IL: Crossway, 2006.

Signountos, James G, and Myron Shank. "Public Roles for Women in the Pauline Church." *JETS* 26:3 (1983) 283–95.

Smyth, John. *The Works of John Smyth*. Vol. 1. Cambridge: Cambridge University Press, 1915.

Sterling, E., Jr. "Women Ministers in the New Testament Church?" *JETS* 19:3 (1976) 209–15.

Strimple, Robert. "The Report of the Minority of the Committee on Women in Church Office," In *Minutes of the Fifty-fifth General Assembly of the Orthodox Presbyterian Church* (1988), 356–73.

Sumner, Sarah. *Men and Women in the Church*. Downers Grove, IL: InterVarsity, 2003.

Swanson, James. *Dictionary of Biblical Languages With Semantic Domains: Greek (New Testament)*. Oak Harbor, WA: Logos Research, 1997.

Swidler, Leonard. *Jesus Was a Feminist*. Lanham, MD: Sheed & Ward, 2007.

Taylor, J. B. "Elders." In *The New Bible Dictionary*. 3rd ed. Downers Grove, IL: InterVarsity, 2004.

Thielman, Frank. *A Theology of the New Testament*. Grand Rapids: Zondervan, 2005.

Thomas, Robert L. *New American Standard Hebrew—Aramaic and Greek Dictionaries*. Anaheim, CA: Foundation, 1998.

Towner, Philip. *The Letters to Timothy and Titus*. NICNT. Edited by Gordon Fee. Grand Rapids: Eerdmans, 2006.

Towner, Philip, and I. Howard Marshall. *A Critical and Exegetical Commentary on the Pastoral Epistles*. New York: Continuum International, 2004.

Tucker, Ruth. *Women in the Maze*. Downers Grove, IL: InterVarsity, 1992.

Van Driel, Neils. "The Status of Women in Contemporary Society: Principles and Practice in Herman Bavinck's Socio-Political Thought." In *Five Studies in the Thought of Herman Bavinck, a Creator of Modern Dutch Theology*, edited by John Bolt. Lewiston, NY: Mellen, 2011.

Walls, A. F. "Deacon." In *The New Bible Dictionary*. 3rd ed. Downers Grove, IL: InterVarsity Press, 2004.

Wallace, Daniel B. "May Women Be Deacons? A Prelude to Dialog." *Bible.org*, June 24, 2004. http://bible.org/article/ may-women-be-deacons-prelude-dialogue.

Walters, James. "'Phoebe' and 'Junia(s)'—Rom 16:1–2, 7." Vol. 1. In *Essays on Women in Earliest Christianity*, edited by Carroll Osburn. Joplin, MO: College Press, 1995.

Waltke, Bruce. *An Old Testament Theology*. Grand Rapids: Zondervan, 2007.

Warfield, Benjamin. "Presbyterian Deaconesses." *Presbyterian Review* 10:38 (1889) 283–93.

White, James R. *Pulpit Crimes: The Criminal Mishandling of God's Word*. Homewood, AL: Solid Ground Christian, 2006.

BIBLIOGRAPHY

———. "Sufficient as Established." In *Perspectives on Church Government: Five Views of Church Polity*, edited by Chad Owen Brand and R. Stanton Norman. Nashville: Broadman & Holman, 2004.

Witherington, Ben, III. *Women in the Earliest Churches*. Cambridge: Cambridge University Press, 1988.

Yrigoyen, Charles, Jr. "The Office of Deacon: A Historical Summary." *Quarterly Review: A Journal for Theological Resources for Ministry* 19:4 (1999) 327–42.